Marie-Louise von Franz

Marie-Louise von Franz, Honorary Patron

Studies in Jungian Psychology by Jungian Analysts

Daryl Sharp,
General Editor and Publisher

MARIE-LOUISE VON FRANZ

The Classic Jungian
and
The Classic Jungian Tradition

Edited by

JAMES A. HALL and DARYL SHARP

INNER CITY BOOKS

For Marie-Louise von Franz and all those who benefited from her presence and teaching

Library and Archives Canada Cataloguing in Publication

Marie-Louise von Franz: the classic Jungian and the classic Jungian tradition / edited by James A. Hall and Daryl Sharp

(Studies in Jungian psychology by Jungian analysts; 122)
Includes bibliographical references and index.

ISBN 978-1-894574-23-5

1. Franz, Marie-Louise von, 1915-1998 2. Jungian psychology.
3. Psychoanalysis I. Hall, James A. (James Albert), 1934-
II. Sharp, Daryl, 1936- III. Series.

BF109.F72M37 2008 150.19'54 C2008-902164-9

INNER CITY BOOKS
Box 1271, Station Q, Toronto, ON M4T 2P4, Canada.
Telephone (416) 927-0355 / Fax (416) 924-1814
Toll-free (Canada and U.S.): Tel. 1-888-927-0355 / Fax 1-888-924-1814
Web site: www.innercitybooks.net / E-mail: booksales@innercitybooks.net

Honorary Patron: Marie-Louise von Franz.
Publisher and General Editor: Daryl Sharp.
Senior Editor: Victoria B. Cowan.
Office Manager: Scott Milligen.

INNER CITY BOOKS was founded in 1980 to promote the understanding and practical application of the work of C.G. Jung.

Cover: Marie-Louise von Franz in her Küsnacht study room (1994).

Printed and bound in Canada by Thistle Printing Company Ltd.

Contents

Editors' Prefaces

There are repetitions in Robert Henderson's interview and my essays on von Franz, also a few elsewhere. I let them stand as written. As far as possible, the style of each contributor has been preserved.

About 1994 von Franz and some others formed a new training institute, the *Centrum* group. Their application to be accredited by the IAAP (International Association for Analytical Psychology) was blocked by the Swiss group of that organization—a major tragedy. I had planned to have a chapter on this, but found no credible author.

This slim book has two goals: first, to honor von Franz and highlight her importance; second, to define the Classic Jungian Tradition (CJT).

Acknowledgments

Three of the papers here, marked * on the Contents page, appeared first, slightly differently, in *Quadrant: Journal of the New York Foundation for Analytical Psychology.*

Abbreviations

Classic Jungian Tradition (CJT)
Developmental Clinical Tradition (DCT)
transcendent function (TF)

unconscious (ucs) & conscious (cs)

transference/countertransference (T/CT).

I am grateful to Alberto Heule, Mary Kroncke, Angela Boone and the indexer.

James A. Hall

*

I have wanted to publish a book in tribute to Marie-Louise von Franz ever since she died. Other tasks intervened, so I was grateful that in the meantime James Hall, my fellow author and colleague, took up the challenge of soliciting and compiling the contributions in this book from eminent others who also considered her the doyenne of Jungian analysts for so many years.

My role in editing and producing this volume has been minor compared to that of Dr. Hall, whose dedication and perseverance in the face of his physical limitations constitute a hero's journey (see below, page 75). I designed the format and cover, corrected obvious errors and compiled the bibliography. Thanks to Victoria Cowan for proofreading, detailed editing and indexing the final page proofs.

I want also to express here my appreciation of the work of Emmanuel Kennedy-Xypolitas of Zürich, von Franz's literary heir, who compiled the magnificent commemorative volume in homage to her, *The Fountain of the Love of Wisdom.*

I must also thank Barbara Davies, who hosted my visits for von Franz's funeral and later times, introducing me to Swiss wonders I will always treasure.

Finally, I take this opportunity to bow to the memory of Edward F. Edinger. He does not figure directly in these pages, but he was certainly a devoted proponent of the CJT for some sixty years until his death in 1998. Some of his publications elucidating Jung's work are listed in the bibliography and final pages of this volume.

Daryl Sharp

Marie-Louise von Franz with C.G. Jung (about 1960).

Introduction

Thomas B. Kirsch, M.D.

Marie- Louise von Franz was perhaps Jung's most visible and creative spokesperson of all the first generation of analysts around him. She was at least a decade younger than most of the others, and so came into prominence later than the others. She met Jung on a school class trip in 1933, as described below by Anne Maguire (page 36).

Marie-Louise von Franz subsequently received a Ph.D. in classics, and in return for helping Jung with Latin and Greek texts, she had analysis with him. For many years her role in the Zürich Jungian world was that of a classics expert. In the 1940s Jung referred patients to her and her analytic career took off from there. She was one of the original seminar leaders when the Zürich C.G. Jung Institute opened (1948), and she quickly became a favorite lecturer. Her own brilliant seminars in the early days, particularly in the 1950s through the 1970s, and her many books and articles have made her—and rightly so—the most important communicator of Jung's basic psychological postulates on the nature of the collective unconscious.

What follows in this introduction is a description of Marie-Louise von Franz by someone who admired her and her work very much, but who had only a distant personal relationship to her. I never had her as an analyst or supervisor, but basically was introduced to her through my parents [analysts James and Jean Kirsch] who knew her well. This is not a typical biographical summary of her life and work, but rather a brief portrait of how she and her work influenced me. I shall present both positive and shadow elements of her personality, which I believe are extremely important in assessing someone as important as von Franz is to the broader Jungian community. Those interested in reading what close intimates have to say about Marie-Louise von Franz will find a cornucopia in *The Fountain of the Love of Wisdom: An homage to Mary-Louise von Franz*, edited by Emmanuel Kennedy-Xypolitas (Chiron publications, 2006).

My own contact with her began in 1953 when she was one of many Jungian analysts from Zürich who came to Los Angeles after World War Two. My parents were instrumental in inviting her at a time when travel from Europe to the United States was prohibitively expensive and not easily done. She seemed like a strict but extremely intelligent schoolteacher. She was already an expert in fairy tales and spoke on that subject.

My next contact came in 1957 and 1958 when I spent two summers in Zürich and audited her lectures on the *puer aeternus* archetype. I was absolutely riveted by her command of the material, and also by how much she seemed to be speaking directly to me. When I began my Jungian training in the early 1960s, I read her lectures on the *puer* in mimeographed form and found them to be one of the most important Jungian books that I had ever read. Today, over forty years later, my opinion about this book is relatively unchanged. Although I would take issue with her emphasis on the neurosis of the *puer,* her description of the behavioral patterns and the archetypal imagery underlying the *puer* complex is profound. Her work on the *puer* archetype greatly extends Jung's description, and she grounds the pattern in clinical practice and numerous dream examples. It is a brilliant exposition.

At the end of the summer of 1958, the first Congress of the recently formed International Association for Analytical Psychology [IAAP] was held in Zürich. My parents attended and after the Congress had dinner with Marlus, as she was known to close friends. I was invited to join them. They were rehashing the Congress and were critically commenting on the changes to the classical Jungian approach, which Michael Fordham was presenting. Since Jung himself was open to Fordham's point of view, his innovations could not be readily dismissed. But it was clear that Marlus did not approve at all of Fordham's views. As a young student I was fascinated by the vehemence of her criticism. She felt that Fordham was no longer Jungian because he did not place the primacy of analytic interpretation on the amplification of archetypal imagery, but rather on how the archetypes are expressed in sexuality and body image in early childhood development.

Gradually her seminars given in English at the Jung Institute were published, and her descriptions of Jung's basic psychological points of view on fairy tales, alchemy, the feminine, the inferior function, and her biography, *C.G. Jung: His Myth in Our Time,* became standard texts for all of us who became Jungian analysts at that time. Utilizing her command of Greek and Latin she continued to study alchemical texts that Jung had begun working on in his lifetime. Prior to his death in 1961 she had been his assistant in this endeavor.

I did not have any further personal contact with her, but I did attend public lectures she gave in both Los Angeles and San Francisco. The audiences were larger each time she returned as her writings became increasingly popular. By the early 1980s she had become the most important spokesperson for Jung's psychology in the world and especially to the English-speaking public.

The developments from Freudian-oriented psychoanalysis, which had initially been introduced by Michael Fordham, gradually spread throughout the Jungian world, eventually influencing the curriculum at the Jung Institute in Zürich. Courses on group therapy, self-psychology, and infant development became part of the Jung Institute curriculum. Von Franz was very critical of the fact that the basic psychology of Jung was being diluted, according to her, by the inclusion of these other subjects. She protested that the spirit of Jung was being lost and began to form an alternative group more focused on her and Jung's writings. In 1994 they broke away to form their own institute, The Research and Training Center in Depth Psychology, where the study of the unconscious, autonomous psyche was central. In many ways the courses offered by this Training Center resembled those at the Jung Institute in the 1950s with an emphasis on amplification of archetypal imagery in dreams and fairy tales. Von Franz was the honorary president until her death in 1998.

My own impression of Marlus was that she was both a brilliant thinker and an equally superb writer, with an uncanny gift for presenting the complicated ideas of Jung in a way that could be understood without simplifying them. She had definite opinions about many things, and her strict adherence to Jung's approach to the collective unconscious was both her great gift and her Achilles' heel. At times one could find her approach to Jung's psychology dogmatic and this prevented an inclusiveness that many of us would have liked to see. Her fate was to give voice to many of Jung's most complicated hypotheses in a way that influenced many people to explore their own unconscious processes.

I do not wish to imply that she was only a communicator of Jung's ideas, because that is not true. All her books and seminars advanced and deepened Jung's ideas in her own unique way. Earlier I mentioned how her research on the *puer* complex greatly expanded our understanding of how that particular archetypal pattern manifests. Her work was extremely creative and furthering of Jungian psychology. What she stated about herself, that her feeling function was inferior to her superior thinking, brought her into conflict in many extraverted outer world situations. A couple of these outer world conflicts have been mentioned above.

In the early 1980s von Franz developed the first symptoms of Parkinsonism, which only became more debilitating as time went on. One can see the early signs of that in the series of films comprising *The Way of the Dream*, which Fraser Boa made with her in the early 1980s.[1] She refused to take medication because she did not want anything to interfere with her dreams. Her dedication to her own development and individuation was admirable, because the limitations that the Parkinsonism imposed were considerable. She was a passionate example of how one can live according to the guiding wisdom of the Self, regulating center of the psyche. She died on February 17, 1998 at the age of 83.

---

[1] This film series is being transferred to DVD. For information please contact G. Chalmers Adams, tel. 416-929-7232; fax 416-929-7225; email: info@gcadams.on.ca—Ed.

PART ONE
Memories and Appreciations

Marie-Louise von Franz while filming *The Way of the Dream* in Zürich (1984).

MARIE-LOUISE VON FRANZ
A Reminiscence

Daryl Sharp

Marie-Louise von Franz saved my life. It's that simple, and that complicated.

I didn't meet her in person until 1976, but already in 1970 her landmark book, *The Problem of the Puer Aeternus,* had opened my eyes to my personal psychology. Well, that's not entirely true; better say she prepared me for what was coming, which is to say that I could appreciate intellectually, with my thinking function, her analysis of the mother-bound man, but I did not truly see its relevance to me—from a feeling standpoint, that is—until I was on my knees three years later. Then her words pierced my heart. Her cogent comments on men who sounded suspiciously like me, devastating as they were to my image of myself at the time, offered an implicit alternative to killing myself.

Needless to say, I took the alternative: I went into analysis. I was in England at the time and my analyst was Dr. Anthony Stevens, a great admirer of von Franz. He helped me to my feet and on his recommendation—and that of the late Irene Champernowne—I was accepted for training at the Zürich Institute. I limped into Zürich in the fall of 1974. Marie-Louise von Franz was my beacon, but alas, she was already fully booked. I shopped around and found another analyst, the late Dr. Richard Pope, who was more than adequate for the likes of me, but that is another story.

As the gods would have it, I then fell in with a shadow companion. Fraser Boa, a charismatic fellow larger than life, had also been accepted as a trainee and was looking for someone to share a house. Fraser had been a teacher for many years before he landed a job as assistant producer on the movie, *Murder on the Orient Express.* He was also Canadian, from London, Ontario, and he too had run out of steam, reached the end of his tether and so on. Our dismal state was echoed by others in training, which is to say we were all there because we had run afoul of our own psychology.

Fraser and I rented a house in the nearby village of Egg. In German this place-name is pronounced Eck, and of course eggs are ubiquitous symbols of new life, which heartened us both. His sister, Marion Woodman, soon joined us. She was just a housewife then, also a former teacher, and quite as neurotic as the rest of us.

Fraser somehow convinced von Franz to take him on. Well, he was that kind of guy; he could sell refrigerators to Eskimos, as the saying goes. Now, my own analyst took a somewhat different approach toward me and my material, bless him, but what I heard from Fraser was at least complementary, and at best an analysis with von Franz, albeit vicariously. Fraser died in 1992 without ever knowing how envious I was when he began to refer to Dr. von Franz as Marlus, the name by which she was known to intimates.

At that time Marie-Louise von Franz was still a frequent lecturer at the Institute on dreams, fairy tales and the symbolic significance of alchemy. At the very first lecture of hers I attended, I was fascinated almost as much by her dirty fingernails as by what she said. My goodness, she was a handsome woman of 58, in the prime of life. I took a liking to her immediately. She had a brilliant smile and was appropriately dressed. Her incisive Logos talk was leavened with Eros. Her English was impeccable. So what about those fingernails? I did not realize back then that my dominant sensation function obliged me to focus on such outer details. Not to mention the fact that my attitude was sadly blinkered, limited to persona perceptions.

Fraser enlightened me. "Marlus loves gardening," he said. "She was probably planting bulbs or weeding before she came to the class, or maybe she just forgot to wash. Whatever. And so what? What you see isn't the sum total of what you get." Oh yeah? This was news to me, but quite typical of what I learned from Fraser, an intuitive for whom time was flexible and boiling an egg was an heroic journey.

During my four years in Zürich, I read everything von Franz had published. Her fairy tale interpretations took my breath away. Some of her lectures had been transcribed and were available from the Institute in mimeographed form. Several were published in the mid-seventies by James Hillman's Spring Publications: *Introduction to the Interpretation of Fairy Tales, The Feminine in Fairy Tales, Shadow and Evil in Fairy Tales, Individuation in Fairy Tales.* I found these and others particularly valuable in amplifying the meaning of images that turned up nightly in my dreams. I devoured them and lamented the fact that they were not indexed. But not for long.

Before I went to pieces I had been a freelance editor, and so I set about creating indexes for these books, as well as for my first love, *The Problem of the Puer Aeternus.* I photocopied my painstaking work and sold it to other students and past graduates. Eventually Spring bought the rights to these indexes and incorporated them in subsequent printings. The benefit to me was twofold: I absorbed von Franz's attitude toward the unconscious and I was able to pay my tuition fees.

I had analytic sessions with Dr. von Franz on two occasions about a year apart. She lived and practiced in Küsnacht, a Zürich suburb, in an unpretentious little house on the side of a hill overlooking the Lake of Zürich—*Lindenbergstrasse* 15. Her housemate was the late Barbara Hannah, whose biographical portrait, *Jung: His Life and Work,* published in 1976, is still among the best. I had heard the story that they lived together because Jung had decreed it on account of the elderly Miss Hannah's failing health. In spite of Miss Hannah's reputation for being cantankerous, I saw only affection between the two.

I remember von Franz's consulting room: simply furnished with a table and straight-backed chair, two comfortable armchairs face-to-face, and overflowing bookshelves. It was the same room she finally died in, which Barbara Davies kindly invited me to view twenty years later, just before the Memorial Service. The only difference I saw was the addition of a single bed and flowers everywhere, giving it the appearance of a shrine. I also recall that she never billed me for those two analytic hours.

In 1976, when it came time for my Propadeuticum, those nerve-wracking mid-term exams at the Institute, I chose Dr. von Franz to test me on the psychological interpretation of fairy tales. I hadn't met her personally yet, though I dare say she knew something of me from Fraser's dreams. It was an oral exam. I was given twenty minutes alone to read the synopsis of a fairy tale. Then I was questioned by my idol, the Expert. In spite of having immersed myself in her work, I didn't do well. I sweated, I coughed, I stuttered; in short, I froze, completely complexed. I could not answer the simplest of questions.

After some twenty minutes, Dr. von Franz sat back and eyed me. "You are truly a mess," she said. "You are either a stupid ninny and shouldn't be here at all, or you have talents as yet undiscovered." On a grading from 1 (tops) to 5 (abysmal), a 3 was a bare pass, which is what she gave me. I crept out of that room feeling deflated but very grateful indeed, for it meant that I could then move on to the next candidate training stage and start seeing clients of my own.

Two years later she examined me again. In the interim I had spent less time frolicking on the Niederdorf, Zürich's nightlife district, and more on why I was where I was. I had re-read von Franz's books and I was intimate with Jung's *Collected Works.* I was as primed for my diploma exam on fairy tales as any horse is for the Kentucky Derby.

I was given a tale from the Grimm collection, "The Crystal Ball," and six hours in which to write a psychological interpretation. I had not read it before, but the motifs were familiar: crystal, eagle, whale, castle, forest, giants, magical hat, wishing, sword, etc., and, wouldn't you know it, an egg within which was the so-called "treasure hard to attain."[2] I wrote my head off and finished in time. The independent examiner refused a mark, saying, "He must have cheated." Von Franz gave me a 1 and penciled a terse note: "He knows his stuff." Of course I was jubilant. I danced all night.

*

In 1978, at the age of forty-two, I returned to Toronto as a certified Jungian analyst. Fraser had been back for a year, and Marion Woodman joined us in 1979. Thanks to the groundwork by laypersons (including the writer Robertson Davies) who had founded the C.G. Jung Foundation of Ontario back in 1970, we three analysts, the first in Canada, all had thriving

---

[2] [Many years later, I dug up this paper and incorporated it into *Not the Big Sleep: On having fun, seriously* (pp. 90ff), the first volume of my **SleepNot Trilogy**.—Sharp.]

practices. Still, I was restless. I had so much energy I thought I might explode. Theoretically it's possible. $E = mc^2$. If you have no place to put your energy it could build up inside until poof!—a burst of flame and at the speed of light you're toast.

For some time I had been trying to interest publishers in my diploma thesis on Franz Kafka, *The Secret Raven: Conflict and Transformation.* I had high hopes. The hundredth anniversary of his birth was coming up, and then the sixtieth anniversary of his death. But there were no takers. I was frustrated. And then Marion and Fraser encouraged me to publish it myself. "Why not?" they said. "You have the tools."

Well, that was true. I knew what was involved in making and marketing a book. Yes, I thought, why not! So I bought the first two Mac computers in Toronto, the other one for my loving partner Vicki, and we went to work. Only I did not fancy being a one-shot vanity press, so I invited manuscripts from other analysts. Marion immediately offered her own diploma thesis, on obesity and anorexia, *The Owl Was a Baker's Daughter.* Fraser helped me design a logo. Then, on a sunny day in May of 1980, I plucked up my courage and called Dr. von Franz at her home in Küsnacht, not forgetting the six-hour time difference.

"Mr. Sharp?" she said. "In Canada? Oh, how are you? I have just come in from the garden. It is a wonderful spring for tulips, don't you think?"

I readily agreed, though I barely knew a tulip from a sunflower.

"Dr. von Franz," I said. "I am starting a publishing house and I'm interested in some of your unpublished seminars. I'm thinking of *Redemption Motifs in Fairy Tales, On Divination and Synchronicity* and *Alchemy: An Introduction to the Symbolism and the Psychology.* I have mimeographed copies."

She said she was very pleased to be asked. What is more, she graciously agreed to be Honorary Patron of Inner City Books. Those three books of hers, published in 1980, have now sold over 100,000 copies, not counting foreign editions in some twenty languages.

In 1983 Fraser got a bee in his own bonnet. "I have an idea," he said. "You can make books; I know how to make films. I will film Marlus on camera interpreting dreams. What do you think about that?"

"Not likely," I scoffed (still a bit jealous about that "Marlus" thing). "No analyst has ever done that, and she won't either."

My skepticism was ill founded. Von Franz agreed to Fraser's project, on condition that the dreams she was to interpret were told on film by the dreamers themselves, not by actors. "Without real dreams told by the actual dreamers," she said, "there is no integrity."

Fraser then founded Windrose Films. I lent him two thousand dollars to get started, which he later told me, when paying me back, was crucial in grounding his vision. He searched out people willing to recount their dreams on camera. He took these to von Franz and filmed her interpreting them. I was agog. The man I had known and loved as a scatter-brained intuitive got all the details right. The result was a stunning ten-hour film series, *The Way of the Dream.* It had its world premier, sponsored by Centerpoint in Cambridge, MA, in 1985. It subsequently had dozens of showings around the world and is currently being transferred to DVD.[3]

Time passed. I published more books. Fraser went on to film a six-hour film series with Joseph Campbell, *This Business of the Gods*. He bought a computer, and with a little help from me

---

[3] See footnote above, p. 13.

on desktop publishing he turned it and *The Way of the Dream* into books. His projects, and mine, were successful beyond our wildest dreams.

Fraser's death from cancer in 1992 was a mighty blow. Von Franz sent a huge bouquet to the church. I mourned his loss, as much as any Enkidu would his Gilgamesh, but I continued to do what was right in front of me. Every six months I sent von Franz a statement of her sales and a check. She once told me that I was the only publisher who ever paid her royalties without being sent a letter from her lawyer—or from Barbara Davies, her writing hand at that time.

Periodically I wrote von Franz asking if she had other manuscripts that Inner City might publish. My persistence was rewarded in 1996 when she offered *Archetypal Patterns in Fairy Tales* and reprint rights to her biography, *C.G. Jung: His Myth in Our Time.* And just six months before she died, she gave Inner City another hitherto unpublished Zürich seminar, *The Cat: A Tale of Feminine Redemption.* These were soon followed, posthumously, by new English editions of *The Problem of the Puer Aeternus* (2000) and her eye-opening commentary on *Aurora Consurgens: A document attributed to Thomas Aquinas on the problem of opposites in alchemy* (2000).

I thought it appropriate that Inner City's hundredth title, published in 2002, was her *Animus and Anima in Fairy Tales,* soon followed by her slim but powerful *The Passion of Perpetua,* which interprets the African martyr St. Perpetua's dreams just before she was fed to the lions in the year 203 A.D.

*

On the morning of February 17, 1998, I awoke to find a message on my answering machine from Chuck Schwartz, an old friend and expatriate Canadian, also an analyst, living in Devon, England. "Von Franz has died," I heard. "I thought you'd like to know." Dear Chuck. He had referred me to Anthony Stevens when I was *in extremis* so long ago. During our time in Zürich, he and I and Fraser and Marion, along with Oblate priest John P. Dourley, were known as the "Canadian Mafia." Years later, when von Franz's beloved bulldog Nibby died of old age, it was Chuck who gifted her a new pup.

There was a similar message via e-mail from Bob Hinshaw, another friend and analyst, publisher of Daimon Books: "Sad news from Zürich. Marlus died early this morning. She has been ailing for quite some time and this was surely her deliverance."

I reeled. Oh no. I thought she would live forever. When I had recovered from this fantasy, I phoned friends and posted notices on the Internet. The response was immediate: heart-felt laments, commiserations to me. More than one correspondent noted yet another passing of the "old guard," those who had worked personally with Jung.

The farewell service was scheduled to be held in the Reform Church of Küsnacht on February 26. I am averse to travel, especially to trips across multiple time zones, and so for a few days I resisted the idea of being there. But in the end I could not *not* go; she was my patron, after all, and the inner urge to publicly honor our association was just too great. And what a joyful occasion it turned out to be: a simple service with three heart-felt valedictory addresses and a Schubert concert, followed by a sumptuous buffet and a seemingly endless supply of Swiss wine, all provided for in advance by von Franz herself. Several hundred of us mingled for hours, consoling each other, greeting old friends and making new ones.

In the midst of all this, I had a sudden realization. This dearly departed old woman, a self-professed thinking type who had often publically confessed her difficulty with her inferior feeling function—to the extent of having to memorize collective expressions of sympathy, congratulations on weddings, etc.—had done this for us. Well, if that does not betoken an integration of opposites, I don't know what does. Thank you, Marlus, I thought, for your generous example of the *coniunctio.*

*

So there it is. The worldwide Jungian community had lost a great lady. I had lost a cherished patron. But the spirit of Marie-Louise von Franz lives on—in her books, in those she worked with analytically, and in the many thousands of others who have been helped or influenced by her writings. Her legacy will surely be that she appreciated Jung's message and did her utmost to further it. And more, for she was not a mindless devotee of Jung. She made her own mark, put her own inimitable stamp both on Jungian psychology and on those she taught.

Personally, I feel privileged and fortunate indeed to be in a position to keep alive the work and spirit of Marie-Louise von Franz, to the benefit of everyone who strives to become psychologically conscious.

Marie-Louise von Franz
Doyenne

Anne Maguire

I am honored to write of my memories of Marie-Louise von Franz, a great lady who died almost ten years ago. She was recognized universally as a *hermeneut,* or interpreter, of the works of Carl Gustav Jung, her tutor, analyst, mentor, and later colleague and always her friend. She will be remembered as an original scholar, a diligent researcher into the nature of psyche, a prolific writer, and also but by no means least, as a devoted caretaker of souls.

She was blessed by the gods indeed, and bestowed with an outstanding excellence of mind and a compassionate but exceedingly humble heart. Throughout the thirty years of our friendship I was ever aware of her innate and ever-present modesty,

It is not possible to briefly do full justice to her genius and the truly adamantine brilliance of her scholarly acumen. Therefore I shall endeavor to portray the living human being I knew. With it comes the hope that this vignette of her life may persuade others to study the nature of her genius, in the life she led and in her works and books. It is a genius of the same ilk as that of C.G. Jung—*Telesphoros*—a being of divine nature who brings to completion.

Her evoked and vivid presence in my conscious thought and in my dreams is that of a warm, genial, amusing and well-related human being. Marie-Louise had an exceptional gift of communication, a gift which enchanted students of all ages and nationalities who attended her splendid, frequently superb, lectures on all the varied aspects of the psychology of Jung, and of her own creative works. I can only describe those lectures as spellbinding. She was deeply admired, but also loved by those who attended her classes at the Institute in Zürich.

In the one-on-one relationship, when she interpreted dreams, her assessment required only a few minutes, after she had listened with serious intent, usually in total silence, to the relating of the dream. It was her complete attention to the matter in hand that unfailingly produced in the recipient a feeling of pleasurable, slightly excited expectancy, as the unique truth of the message from the Self unfolded. (She did say once that she had analyzed over 60,000 dreams, and not a single one was a repetition.)

She was a master analyst because she truly cared that what she wished to convey to her analysands was absolutely clear to them. In this respect she did not suffer "foolishness" gladly. In the analytical situation the dream was always central and she sought its meaning assiduously in dialogue with the dreamer.

In later years she would ask me when I arrived in her presence, "Have you a dream"? Keep in mind that the first dream brought to the first analytic session is always considered to be important, indeed vital, as a symbolic foreshadowing of the dreamer's subsequent path. Later it is referred to as the "initial" or "original" dream.

Marie-Louise had a propensity to lift one's spirits. After an hour or even a few minutes with her, one felt less weighed down, stepped more lightly on this earth. She hated to appear unkind and sometimes became anxious regarding her feeling function that she claimed was inferior. I never found her to be so, never saw an unkindness in her.

Her generosity of heart did sometimes overtax her and

eventually took a toll of her energies at the expense of her health. But even in her later years her intellectual assessments were always delivered with a warm relatedness that was unique to her.

How did I meet her? This can only be answered by asking another question. How did I become an analyst? A brief explanation is required.

One cold autumn morning about forty years ago now I found myself alone in a vast Basilica in the far West of France. The church was dedicated to St. Anne, mother of the Virgin Mary and patron saint of France. She is believed to have taught the Virgin to read. Her sainthood is celebrated on July 26, also the birth date of Carl Gustav Jung in 1875.

Two years prior to this event I had been browsing in a bookshop in the *Rue de la Paix* in Paris, searching for a Simenon thriller. Suddenly I was subjected to a bombardment by a book that fell upon me from a higher shelf. I put it back, but although it seemed to have been placed securely it fell on my head again. I then opened it and found it to be written by C.G. Jung. I was on the point of replacing it yet again, but decided to glance through it. It seemed odd to me that such a thing should happen twice. The paragraph that caught my attention was about the spiritual nature of women. I bought the book for the sum of thirty-four francs and on that day my life changed forever.

From late afternoon until dawn next day I read the book. Then I fell asleep and dreamed. In the dream a beautiful golden dog with golden eyes came to lead me to the future. It took me some years to discover that the mighty Zeus himself had a dog with golden eyes. I went home and read everything I could find written by Dr. Jung. He had died several years earlier and the works were then being published in English. I became deeply immersed in his ideas, in dreams and in myths. I began to observe and take note of my own dreams, many of which were of alchemists, where I was in laboratories or ancient houses with them. I found these dreams strange and disturbing.

As an act of thanksgiving, so to speak, I had gone to the Basilica of St. Anne to offer my gratitude for the unusual and fateful introduction to the works of Dr. Jung. As I sat alone in that vast church in the early morning of that bleak day, suddenly from nowhere appeared a small black and white terrier dog that joined me. He jumped up on the pew beside me and immediately licked both my hands. Later he followed me to the altar and then I asked him, as he stroked my hand, what did he want? In the subsequent silence I was assailed by the thought that I should go at once to Zürich to see the house where Dr. Jung had lived and died. Immediately the little dog disappeared and I never saw him again. His task as *psycho-pompos* had been completed. I got up and within an hour I was on my way to Zürich via Paris.

I arrived in the late afternoon at the door of the C.G. Jung Institute in the *Gemeindestrasse*, to learn that that Dr. Jung had never lived in that house. The splendid secretary, on learning that I was a physician and had read Jung's works, suggested that I should return the following day to meet Dr. Franz Riklin, president of the Institute. I hasten to add that in the course of my Jungian studies in the period before I found myself in Zürich, I had not been aware of the existence of such an Institute in that city. So I was surprised because I knew nothing whatsoever regarding the world of analysts and their training practice. A study of analytical disciplines had not been part of my own medical training, although I had been trained at prestigious medical schools in both London and Paris. At that time the importance of the psyche and its mysteries had not yet penetrated into the domain of medical consciousness. So I had not encountered Jung's psychology or theories until the book fell upon my head.

When this event occurred I was already a specialist-physician and dermatologist. In the latter discipline I had observed early on and had intuited that the majority of skin diseases possessed a psychic etiology. This knowledge had occupied my thoughts for some time; but was not then nor is it today an established concept of the universal philosophical background of the etiology of dermatological disease. (According to medical teaching even today, the etiology of most skin diseases is unknown). I was therefore not unaware of the connection between psyche and soma, or of the importance of a psychosomatic approach, which I had begun to use in my capacity as a skin specialist even though it was contrary to the general trend of the times.

A day or so after my arrival in Zürich, I met with Dr. Franz Riklin for three hours. We discussed the events that had directed my footsteps to Zürich, and also my strange alchemical dreams as well as my interest in the psychic aspect of medicine. The upshot of that meeting occurred about two months later when I returned to Zürich to enter into analysis with Dr. Riklin, and to consider undergoing training to become an analyst. Because of my own work and the demands of his position as president of the Institute, Dr. Riklin suggested that I should also analyze with Miss Barbara Hannah, who was incidentally English like myself. It was a good arrangement. Dr. Riklin trained as a surgeon but underwent specialized training later as a psychiatrist with Professor H. Maier at the Burgholzli Clinic in Zürich, and then dedicated himself entirely to the psychology of C.G. Jung. Dr. Riklin's mother was a cousin of C.G. Jung and Dr. Riklin himself had spent a great deal of his youth in Dr. Jung's house. Miss Hannah had had a personal analysis with Dr. Jung.

In my analysis I learned from both my analysts that the dream and its interpretation were central. It is unsettling for me today when I hear that sometimes in current Jungian practice the dream is no longer central and sometimes is not analyzed. I also learned from Dr. Riklin the absolute reality of the unconscious mind, an idea I had already encountered in the books by Jung that I had studied. From Barbara Hannah I learned the value of active imagination and I began to practice it with her as teacher.

It was Miss Hannah who introduced me to Marie-Louise von Franz. The two ladies lived in the same house, and each had her own analytical practice there. Seemingly several years previously, both of them at exactly the same time had to find a new home and Dr. Jung suggested that they should share a house. He thought, apparently, that it was good for an analyst to have a companion with whom to share discussions of on-going problems arising from the work, as well as general events. Barbara was a generation older than Marie-Louise, so at the beginning of their relationship they had considerable difficulties in adjusting to each other. Later, though, they became very close friends. It was in fact Barbara who told me of the immense creativity of Marie-Louise and of her great admiration for her.

Left to right: Barbara Hannah, M. Esther Harding, Marie-Louise von Franz
(about 1960)

Franz Riklin had described Barbara Hannah as a master analyst and it was true. However sometimes she found my dreams difficult so she asked me if I minded if Marie-Louise analyzed them. I did not mind at all, and thus I became privy to the wizardry of the dream interpretations of Marie-Louise. It was phenomenal, and she was outstanding. Her insight was aided by a monumental knowledge of myth and fairy tales, and also medicine. After she analyzed my first alchemical dream she invited me to supper with Barbara and herself and that was the beginning of our friendship.

I am reminded of a statement made by Dr. Dieter Baumann, the grandson of Dr. Jung, who wrote in an obituary of Franz Riklin the following words: "Acceptance of the unconscious goes hand-in-hand with respect for the personality through which the unconscious manifests itself, be it one's own personality or that of the other person."[4] This supports the fact that Dr. Riklin devoted himself entirely to the psychology of C.G. Jung, which is based on the reality of the unconscious.

I always felt extremely at ease with both my regular analysts, and also with Marie-Louise von Franz when she analyzed my dreams from time to time. Later, she was to explain that in some way my alchemical dreams were related to my work in the psychosomatic sphere of medicine, and she encouraged me to work deeper in that field. I found that each of the three analysts with whom I worked stressed the absolute reality of the unconscious, the importance of the dream as pivotal in the analysis, ever to be regarded essentially as a message from the Self. Dr. Riklin spoke to me often of the complex and neuroses theories, and frequently of the Word Association test with its unparalleled value in certain cases.

---

[4] "A Memory of Franz Riklin," in *Spring 1970*, p. 1.

Both Miss Hannah and Dr. von Franz supported amplification and I learned, then, that to understand the unconscious one had to learn the language of the symbol. From each analyst I learned that the recognition of the opposites and the shadow personality with its contrasexual aspect was the bedrock of the analytical process prior to the understanding and consequent withdrawal of subjective projections as had been taught by Jung.

Less than two years after the commencement of my analysis with Dr. Franz Riklin, his sudden and untimely death on August 1, 1969, brought an abrupt ending of our work together. This very sad loss was a great shock to me and to all of his many friends.

I continued to work with Barbara Hannah until I secured my diploma, but she remained my friend and mentor until her death. From Barbara I learned a good deal of Dr. Jung's life and work. Every day in the summer she placed a fresh rose on the mantel in the dining room so that his memory was ever alive. In our conversations about him I found that both Barbara and Marie-Louise always discussed his work in great detail and with exactitude so that I would remember it in relationship to the man as he was. Marie-Louise was ever the teacher. She was a good cook, and always explained a dish or a wine so that one would remember it. The houses were ordered, quiet and peaceful, both in Küsnacht and in Bollingen. Both were always guarded by Marie-Louise's bulldogs. The first one, whom she adored, was "Nibby," a shortened form of 'His Nibs," because he was Winston Churchill III by name. The second one was a lovely little female called Laura; in spite of her slightly nervous disposition at first, she became a true friend for her mistress.

The illness of Marie-Louise had already presented itself before Barbara's death on September 4, 1986. Afterward,

Marie-Louise decided to continue to live in the home in Küsnacht that they had shared for so long. She had a companion and nurses to care for her, and she was surrounded by friends. For some years she was still able to spend summers in Bollingen, in the house she had built in the forest. It was a place of infinite charm deep in Nature where she was content, and where over the years she had dispensed such generous hospitality to so many friends. Also it was where both she and Barbara had undertaken their respective creative works. Barbara's biographical memoir, *Jung: His Life and Work,* is a splendid book.

Now I would like to mention certain events that appear to be important markers during von Franz's life journey.

1. 1933

When she was eighteen years old Marie-Louise visited the garden of C.G. Jung with friends from school. Dr. Jung told the young people present that he had a young woman patient who "lived on the moon." Marie-Louise was utterly shocked and could not accept the remark. So she asked Dr. Jung if he meant that it was "as if" the girl lived on the moon. He said, "No, it is not 'as if.' She *did* live on the moon." It was on that day that Marie-Louise realized there are two levels of reality. She perceived another world as real as the one she knew, and that dreams and myths are as present as the physical realm.

She came to understand the overwhelming importance of a dream as a message from that inner world, and its absolute reality. It was a revelation that never left her consciousness. She told me that when she realized there was another reality level she simply could not take it in at first. Then she grasped that Jung meant that what happens psychologically is the real reality. This was a revelation for her. When Jung says nothing happens by chance he speaks a great truth, or he speaks with the Spirit of Truth. This was the first time she had met anyone who spoke so quietly and firmly, and with complete conviction, of the presence of another world other than our so-called objective reality.

2. The Dream of the Greek Gods

Still in her eighteenth year, she began to wonder what to do on leaving school. In her quandary she had a dream—she was sitting on the steps of the Acropolis in Greece, with a knapsack between her knees, and no money. Suddenly in the sunshine (Apollo) she saw all the Olympic gods entering in a long procession. They approached with hands held out begging. She opened her sack and wanted to give them something, but she had nothing except a loaf of bread. So she cut it into pieces and gave each god a piece, apologizing by saying, "I am sorry but this is all I have."

After this dream she decided to study ancient classical languages, because the gods wanted something from her. Zeus, his wife Hera, Hermes and Aphrodite. Just imagine! It is a breathtaking dream. Imagine to be visited and asked for something by the gods! What did she have that they wanted?

I always felt this dream set the stage for her whole life. To her credit and even greater humility she never appropriated the mantle of power. She always remained modest and kind. In youth she connected with Hermes. But she told me that later in life it was Aphrodite who became dominant.

From her writing pattern it would seem she always followed the stream of life. She appears to have consistently sought the place where there was a nucleus of energy, and that meant a concentration of life. She worked incredibly hard and when her creative genius beckoned—when she had a hunch, an interest, or a curiosity—she was obliged to follow.

3. The Dream of the Untrodden Ground

One day, almost *en passant*, she mentioned that when she was young she had a strange dream. In the dream she walked on ground where no other feet had trodden before. She felt herself to be walking on earth that had never supported human feet. I thought it was oracular, so I discussed it with Barbara Hannah who knew of it. She related it to Marie-Louise's already immense and original work and the work to come. Later I was to learn of Jung's warning that in new fields of research into the deep psyche, there is innate danger for the explorer.

One afternoon some months before Marie-Louise died, I went out to Bollingen where she was alone with a nurse-companion. Although frail, her mind was clarity itself. There in Bollingen she gave me to read the finished manuscript of her magnificent book on the Spirit of Eros as lived by the ancient Shi-ite alchemist, Mohammed Ibn Umail. The book is called *Hall Ar-Rumuz* (Clearing of Enigmas). The foreword is by Professor Theo Abt who aided her by doing so much to track down obscure alchemical texts in Hyderabad. She had already discovered that Aquinas was versed in the work of Mohammed Ibn Umail, the Arabic alchemist, whilst researching *Aurora Consurgens: A document attributed to Thomas Aquinas on the problem of opposites in alchemy.*

Alchemy, as we have learned, is the science that allows the spirit of matter to speak, and whose highest goal is the *coniunctio.* The connection between the Song of Solomon, Mohammed Ibn Umail, (the alchemist), and St. Thomas (the Christian) together with his soul (Sophia), and not least by any means, the questing spirit of Marie-Louise herself, combined with her pure Eros, fuses into a perfect whole in the time span of one thousand years. The *Aurora* is a masterwork, and so is *Hall Ar-Rumuz.* Once when I was discussing the book with her secretary, Dr. Barbara Davies, she told me that Marie-Louise believed that alchemy will be the mediating element in a reconciliation between Islam and Christianity.

Again in 1974, she produced a book born out of deep study on her part, *Number and Time.* The subject was the linkage between psyche and matter, which is central in alchemy. Almost twenty years earlier, in 1958, Dr Jung had already seen Number as an archetypal reality participating in both the material and the spiritual world, and potentially bridging them.[5] It became the task of Marie-Louise von Franz to prove this theory.

In *Number and Time,* she opens a new perspective as she explains the significance of number as a link between psyche and matter. After this work she continued the exploration with numbers in connection with synchronicity itself *(On Divination and Synchronicity: The Psychology of Meaningful Chance).* A synchronistic event occurs at an unpredicted moment in time when psyche (which in its deepest layers is not bound to time) and matter (which is linked to the world of time) unite in a noncausal way. She concluded that the common meaning that cannot be foreseen is the element always linked to the sporadic union of psychic and physical events. *Number and Time* is a book of great magnitude and is the container of a profound truth, important in the ongoing understanding of the mysterious connection between psyche and matter that has occupied the mind of humanity for centuries. Sitting there in her bedroom in

---

[5] See "Flying Saucers: A Modern Myth," *Civilization in Transition,* CW 10, par. 778.

Bollingen as she was nearing the end of her life, I perceived the great depths to which she had explored the unconscious world "where no feet had trodden before." In this work she risked her life.

Marie Louise von Franz was a wise woman who brought consciousness to countless individuals and groups worldwide, through personal contact and through her many books. She lived her life as a unique being. I was indeed fortunate and blessed to know her in life and to become her friend.

On February 26, 1998, I was invited to speak at her funeral service by Gotthilf Isler of Zürich, her friend and colleague. I append below the words I used to speak of my friend that sad day when the world became a poorer place without her.

Valediction at the Funeral Service of Marie-Louise von Franz, February 26, 1998

I am deeply honored to have received the invitation to deliver this valedictory address for our dear departed friend, Marie-Louise von Franz, a truly great lady whose passing is sadly marked by those of us gathered here today. A day when the reality of our loss is realized as we bid her earthly self adieu.

I doubt not that each one of us here has had his or her life transformed in some way, either by personal contact or through knowledge of her writings, which in turn have introduced her to a vast world audience.

She was born at a momentous time, in the first terrible winter of the Great War, in the German city of Munich, itself a city under the aegis of the little hooded *kabir,* the *Munchener kindt,* the child. This cloaked figure was akin to the phallic *kabir* of the Ancient world—*Telesphoros,* a companion and guide of *Asklepios,* the god of medical healing. At the same time, he was the youthful double of *Asklepios,* and was known as "the one who brings to completeness," the god of inner transformations.

Three years after her birth, toward the end of the war, she was brought to Switzerland by her Austrian parents. Eventually she became a Swiss citizen and lived her life here. At the age of 18 years, one afternoon in 1933, the year Adolph Hitler seized power in Germany, she was invited by a friend to meet Carl Gustav Jung. The meeting was portentous, for on that day she was introduced to the reality of another realm—the hidden inner world. As the unconscious presented itself to her through the medium of Dr. Jung she was utterly astounded. During that afternoon Jung had described a young woman he had treated who "lived on the moon." When Marie-Louise heard this, she decided to approach the professor and ask him if he meant that it was "as if" the girl lived on the moon. Dr. Jung answered that it was not "as if," but that the girl did live on the moon. She told me that at that moment she thought "either he is crazy or I am." That meeting circumscribed the fateful moment of transformation in her life. The following year, 1934, she began to work with C.G. Jung, and did so until his death in 1961.

The statement made by Jung, which had so perplexed her, led to a lifelong search for the inner truth as concealed in the unconscious world of the objective psyche. She learned of the importance of the dream as a message from that interior world. She had a splendid incisive intellect that enabled her to become a deep and later an inspirited and inspiriting thinker. Her ability to grasp and to discern had a rapier-like character. Yet she was always able to explain a point or enlarge an aspect of the problem with an exquisite but immensely patient clarity. This aspect of her personality belongs to the archetype of the teacher for she was, in my view, unassailable in that particular field. She retained, it seems, this lucid clarity of mind until she died.

As a multilinguist and Medieval Latin scholar, she collaborated with Jung in the study of alchemy and contributed related studies to two of his major works, *Aion* and *Mysterium Coniunctionis.* In her early years as an analyst she dreamed she was walking on ground where "no one had trodden before." Some time later she was to begin her monumental creative work on fairy tales, and later with the archetypal world of numbers. These previously unexplored fields were to occupy her energies for many years.

For a moment I would like to speak of the fairy-tale studies. Today they are so much a part of Jungian training and psychotherapy that one forgets the immense primary work undertaken by Marie-Louise in those early years. As a young woman she enjoyed the natural world, particularly the mountains where she liked to walk in summer and ski in winter. She liked nothing better than to be immersed in nature with the greenness of its trees, the flowers under foot, and the splendid mountains themselves. She had an exceptional knowledge of animal lore, and a profound sympathy with that world. She held the present view that the natural world is in fact doomed by humanity's gross unconsciousness and the ignorance of the spirit of wild nature. A spirit, which if left alone, could and indeed would bring about a reparation of the damage to which the earth and its seas has already been subjected, but only if left alone by humans.

With such vital interests as the importance of the dream in an individual life, and the domination of the spirit in the natural world, it is clear that the domain of fairy tales, those age-old traditional tales should call to her. She answered the call and was seized by the material. She read thousands of stories from all over the world. This empowered her to perceive those hidden secrets held in them, which engendered their fascination. Thus she came to understand perhaps better than anyone else in the world the archetypal structure of the natural world in these tales and in the unconscious psyche. She saw, as it were, the skeletal structure of psyche, much perhaps as one sees the singular distinctive skeletal shape and pristine beauty of a deciduous tree in winter time, without its leaves. I am sure that this immense work and the knowledge thus gained from her creative genius led her to become a master analyst and an incomparable interpreter of dreams.

There was however another aspect to her multifaceted personality, an aspect seldom immediately apparent because of her innate modesty and her primarily introverted attitude. She had a dislike for what was ostentatious and power driven, and thus her Eros had a certain quality of reticence. In her lectures one was always aware that behind her powerful intellect her Eros was, albeit shyly, constantly palpably present. I always thought her Eros to be totally genuine, all-pervading and enveloping: the true *caritas*. She was a very kind woman, and real love has much to do with kindness.

In her attitude toward others it seemed to me that she desired that all should benefit from her knowledge and experience which she offered freely and generously, just as she gave her hospitality to many. She endeavored to aid others to reach the hidden inner truth as she perceived it to be. This was the sprit by which she lived, always seeking to bring a soul to the light of illumination. I believe it is because of this true kindness that we have come gladly to remember her today with our love, despite deep sadness at our loss.

In the last years she bore a devastating physical illness stoically, nobly, and with immense courage. She was indomitable right up until the end of her earthly life. In spite of her suffering she retained her richly perceptive insights, her capacity for trenchant asides, her kindness, and last but by no means least, her sense of humor. It astonished me how, disabled in body, in noticeable pain, and sometimes with the speech difficulties that accompanied her illness she was able to joke and to laugh with abandon, and to express herself in her own inimitable way.

During one dark evening not very long ago, after we had discussed the *unus mundus,* she told me she had had a wonderful dream the night before. In it her illness was cured and had left her completely healed in body. She told me she was immensely happy in the dream, and she added that she would be leaving soon. The dream brought her great joy.

She strove throughout the years of her tribulation to participate consciously in her individual pathway to wholeness, as it unfolded in her dreams and outer life. I see her as a woman who ever sought the inner spirit of creative truth and fought for justice in the acceptance of that truth.

This is the spirit that gathers us together today; we, the many friends who loved her; those who accompanied her both in her prime and during her years of travail. In particular I would like to mention those nursing companions, faithful, devoted and tireless in their love, who served her so well and eased her passage from this life.

I also would like to mention those who contributed to her comfort in diverse ways. With respect I mention Dr. Barbara Davies, friend, assistant and collaborator, who became her writing hand; and others who each helped in their own way: Julia Brunner, Alison Kappes, Nomiki Kennedy, Vicki Reiff, Mary Scheiner, Regina Schweitzer-Vullers, Zita Tauber and her sister Marie-Anne von Franz. I felt she would have liked to die in Bollingen which she loved. But that was not God's will and so she died in her town house with all the good spirits of her past, and of her students, analysands and many friends who came to see her. Not forgetting her late dear companions, Barbara Hannah and Franz Riklin, and their regular gatherings together at that house.

I am very sorry that my dear friend of over thirty years Marie-Louise von Franz has died. She leaves the world a poorer place and although in the years to come undoubtedly some will endeavor to match her, they shall surely fail because no one will possess the unique combined attributes contained in the creative genius of this great lady.

Because of her love and reverence for the soul, may I with

respect quote a few lines from the beautiful poem "Ode to the Soul" by the great Islamic physician-philosopher Ibn Sina (Avicenna) who died a thousand years ago.

> Out of her lofty home she hath come down, upon thee
> This white dove in all the pride of her reluctant beauty:
> Veiled is she, from every eye, eager to know her, though
> In loveliness unshrouded radiant, unwillingly she came,
> And yet perchance still more unwilling to be gone from
>   thee—
> So she is torn by griefs.
> ....
> Why then was she cast down from her high peak: to
> This degrading depth?
> God brought her low. But for a purpose-wise,
> That is concealed even from the keenest mind
> And the liveliest wit.
> And if the tangled mesh impeded her
> The narrow cage denied her wings to soar freely
> In heaven's high ranges, after all she was a
> Lightening flash that brightly glowed—
> Momently o're the tents and then was hid
> As though its gleam was never glimpsed below.[6]

Postscript (2008)

It is almost half a century since the death of Dr. C.G. Jung, and there now remain few practicing analysts who were trained by him. They are known as classic Jungian analysts. Today, in the natural order of things, considerable changes have occurred in many aspects of Jungian thought, but particularly in that of the analytic process. These changes are not always acceptable to those of us who were trained in the immediate years after

---

[6] A.J. Arberry, ed. and trans., *Persian Poems*.

Jung's death.

Before her own death, Marie-Louise von Franz told me that Dr. Jung reflected for almost a year upon the correct manner by which an analyst trained by him should be addressed. He decided eventually that the term *analytical psychologist* should be applied to those who had undergone the system of training he had advocated. The reason was that he wanted to make it clear that an analyst did actually analyze the contents of the deep psyche. He did not therefore accept the Freudian term psychoanalyst, nor the more recent and popular term psychotherapist as suitable for his in-depth exploration of the unconscious. This fact is important and should be remembered. Such exploration also requires that the language of the symbol must be learned by the analyst. Naturally this is a monumental task but it is vital. The careful consideration that Jung applied in the choice of a correct professional term for the analyst reflects the same attention and thought he gave to every aspect of his work in the development of his psychology.

It must be remembered that the unconscious is really unconscious and a danger may arise if this fact is forgotten or not realized. It is then that one must bring to mind Dr. Jung's somber reminder that the reality of the inner world is the true psychological reality because of the fact that in certain respects it not only perceives more than consciousness but even exerts a moral authority over conscious actions. If the dreams of both the analyst and the analysand are then examined with serious intent, bearing in mind the true psychological reality, possible dangers may be avoided in the transference situation and other problems that may arise.

It should above all be realized that although life ever presents dangers of every description, the wisdom of the deep psyche may be grasped by analysis of and understanding of the humble dream.

In the overwhelming technological explosion of our age, with the parallel rise of mass-mindedness. there is increasing danger of a universal diminution of conscious awareness, whereby it becomes difficult to remember that the unconscious is really unconscious. In this time of grave danger, one may recall the wisdom of Jung.

I think Dr. C.G. Jung was one of the great if not the greatest exploratory pioneers into the soul of mankind. Therefore I see no valid reason to decry, demean or reject out of hand certain aspects of his analytic approach, which unfortunately seems to have occurred in certain areas since his death.

In view of the scientific nature of Jung's work and his exceptional and constant exactitude in the formulations of his principles, it might be advisable for those who do not concur entirely with his approach to the psyche, or purport to go beyond it, to reflect on their comparative littleness.

Finally, even though a decade has passed since Marie-Louise von Franz left this earth, we may still direct our gratitude toward her beloved memory. She remains one of the foremost interpreters of Jung's work and has made it possible for the actuality of his genius to be recognized universally. Yet, at the same time we honor her own creative nature and the way she herself explored the most profound psychic depths to further increase our understanding of the vast unknown inner world.

Marie-Louise von Franz, 1915-1998.

Marie-Louise von Franz in front of her tower at Bollingen. She cut her own wood for the fireplace where all meals were cooked.

Marie-Louise von Franz
Her Life and Work

Barbara Davies

In this essay I attempt to provide a brief outline of the life and work of Marie-Louise von Franz. The choice of themes is subjective, based both on the books of Dr. von Franz and on private discussions with her.

Early Years

Marie-Louise von Franz was born in Munich on January 4, 1915, during the First World War. At the time, her father, Baron Erwin von Franz, served as a Staff colonel in the Austro-Hungarian army. Marie-Louise and her elder sister, Marie-Anne, stayed with their mother in the south of Germany. At the end of the war, the family moved to Switzerland. Her parents remained Austrian and their daughters would have done the same but for the fact that by 1936 Hitler's pressure on Austria had become so dangerous that the two sisters applied for Swiss citizenship. Just before Hitler's army marched into Austria, in 1938, both sisters were granted Swiss nationality.

Even in childhood, stimulated by her keen mind and genuine interest in nature, Marie-Louise von Franz began to experiment with matter. One of her first efforts was to boil the resin of pine trees and watch what happened, hoping it would be transformed into amber. While it was being heated, the contents of the little pot carbonized, causing black smoke to fill the kitchen. Her parents' lack of enthusiasm compelled the young alchemist to give up that experiment.

A Fateful Encounter Sparks the Creative Process

Shortly before she graduated from high school, Marie-Louise von Franz was introduced to C.G. Jung, who was fifty-eight years old at the time. In exchange for analysis, which she could not otherwise afford, von Franz agreed to translate classic Greek and Latin texts that Jung needed for his research in alchemy. One day, while she was plowing through alchemical works from the sixteenth century, Jung walked in and asked her to decipher a handwritten text of the thirteenth century—seemingly ascribed to St. Thomas Aquinas—entitled *Aurora Consurgens*. Acknowledging her talents, Jung also suggested that she write a commentary to this work. This took her fifteen years to complete. During this period of intensive work she also wrote *The Passion of Perpetua* (1949), an exposition on the visions of the early Christian martyr, St. Perpetua, and on the transformation of the God-image in the collective unconscious psyche of that time. She also finished her studies of classical philology at the University of Zürich with a doctoral thesis, *A Scientific Analysis of the Concept of Aesthetics as Described in the Iliasscholia* (1943, unpublished to date), and completed two volumes, amounting to almost two thousand pages, on the symbolism of fairy tales (1952, 1953).[7]

Also during this period Jung asked Dr. von Franz to visit the Vatican library in order to study the writing of St. Thomas Aquinas and, if possible, trace any other alchemical treatises he might have written. The first days at the library went smoothly

---

[7] [Von Franz undertook this research on behalf of the author, Hedwig von Beit, whose book *Symbolik des Marchen: Versuch einer Deutung* was published without acknowledging von Franz's massive contribution.—Ed.]

when she was given access to the manuscripts. But soon enough, one of the librarians asked her why she needed these texts. Marie-Louise von Franz explained that she was reading a text called *Aurora Consurgens* which she believed to be an alchemical treatise, and that she was keenly interested in Arabic alchemy. When she went to continue her reading the following day, she was informed that the texts she wanted could not be found. Disheartened, she returned to Zürich.

In the early nineties, Dr. von Franz received new evidence that confirmed her long-standing hypothesis that St. Thomas was indeed the author of the alchemical treatise *Aurora Consurgens. The Aurora*, as Dr. von Franz always referred to it, was written in a state of ecstasy at death's door. It discloses Thomas Aquinas' visionary encounter with the soul in the form of Sophia. The treatise seems to have roots in the Biblical Song of Solomon, which according to historical reports St. Thomas was interpreting as death came upon him. Dr. von Franz points out that clearly the treatise shows that the author was well versed in Arabic alchemy, particularly in the writing of the tenth-century Shi-ite mystic and alchemist, Mohammed ibn Umail. Of all the books she wrote, the commentary to the *Aurora* (1957) meant the most to her and was the book of which she was most proud. In the last decade, Dr.von Franz devoted much of her time to the writings of Mohammed ibn Umail and the spirit of Eros as lived by this ancient Shi-ite alchemist, exemplified in his masterwork *Hall Ar-Rumuz* (Clearing of Enigmas).

Marie-Louise von Franz never tired of insisting on the importance of alchemy, the science that allows the spirit of matter to speak and has the *coniunctio* as its highest goal. As she saw it, the reconciliation between Islam and Christianity is a future task in which alchemy will be the mediating element.

Is it a matter of synchronicity that the number 17, which was the date of her death and the number she interpreted as symbolizing the completion of individuation and the realization of an individual's uniqueness, is also a most highly-venerated number in Shi-ite mysticism?

Aspects of her Private Life

Marie-Louise von Franz became a world-renowned lecturer and was one of the foremost supporters of the C.G. Jung Institute of Zürich when it was founded in 1948. She took Jung's advice to share her life and home with Barbara Hannah. This precious friendship, deeply meaningful to both ladies, lasted until Miss Hannah died in 1986.

Marie-Louise loved to stay in her tower at Bollingen, for this was the place where she felt in tune with the spirit of nature. Jung had suggested that she buy the land and have a tower built on it. Her hermitage, intentionally without modern conveniences such as electricity and a flushing cistern, is hidden by the forest from which von Franz fetched wood to heat and cook. Close to the tower, a moor pond, abundant with yellow lilies, evokes the feeling of eternal existence.

Insights

Not long before she died I had the opportunity to talk with Dr. von Franz about her enormous engagement with fairy tales. Her aim, she explained, was never practical. She abhorred the idea of using fairy tales to bring about rational understanding. This she felt was blasphemous and a misunderstanding of the deeper message fairy tales convey. Dealing with the living spirit is an excruciating experience, she confided, clarifying for me that the agonizing process she went through with each interpretation was what produced the light she gave to us.

In another conversation about the mother complex in

general, Dr. von Franz stated that recent dreams gave her reason to believe that this complex can be redeemed. "*Ein Zeitgeschehen,*" she remarked, which means "in its own time." The problems of our time, such as growing collectivism, misdirected materialism, and a lack of understanding of the symbolic, caused her deep worry. With unflinching awareness, Marie-Louise von Franz listened to the dreams of the people around her right up to the last day of her life. She thought that our idea of consciousness is naïve. In her opinion, we mainly believe in the reality of visible matter. The other reality is transcendent and has still to be investigated. Dr. von Franz was certain that dreams will give us the clues we need.

Marie-Louise von Franz loved to speak of St. Niklaus von Flue ("Brother Klaus") as the patron of psychotherapy. People like Klaus, who suffer their process of individuation more deeply and consciously than the surrounding collective, are elevated to an archetypal dimension and transformed into the "*Anthropos*-image." In *The Visions of Bruder Klaus* (1959), Dr. von Franz shows that the Self was the guide that led the Swiss saint to his preordained spiritual destiny and the bearing of his particular cross, whose ultimate meaning aimed at the unification of psychic opposites.

Honors

The following anecdote describes how much respect Dr. von Franz earned and deserved in the view of many people. Dr. Franz Riklin, at that time president of the C.G. Jung Institute and a colonel in the Swiss army, organized a course in 1965 entitled "Attack and Defense." This was to be attended by several officers of the medical corps of the Swiss army. For this occasion, Colonel Riklin invited Dr. von Franz to give a speech which was to take place on the main square in the village of Sachseln. Dr. Riklin arranged for Marie-Louise von Franz and her dog, Nibby, to be fetched in Küsnacht and driven to Sachseln where a military parade with fanfare and officials were waiting. As they arrived four officers dashed to open the doors of the military Volkswagen to let Dr. von Franz and her dog out. After a small incident caused by Nibby when he barked at the military band, Marie-Louise von Franz and her dog solemnly proceeded to review Colonel Riklin's regiment. Thereafter she delivered a most impressive speech, "Nike and the Waters of the Styx," to the gathered assembly. This talk can be found in her book, *Archetypal Dimensions of the Psyche* (1997).

Scientific Research

In talking about her book, *Psyche and Matter* (1992), which addresses a subject that had been of great concern to her throughout her life, Marie-Louise von Franz mentioned recent dreams that dealt with the fact that inorganic matter precedes organic matter. "The thought is not difficult, but the consequences are tremendous," she said. According to her, we reject the concept of animated matter, forgetting that it too is an aspect of the reality of the psyche. She calls upon us to study the relations of psyche and matter and to view them as two complementary cosmic principles.[8]

Marie-Louise von Franz had already paved the road for this task with *Number and Time* (1974), an opus of unequalled insight and genius. According to C.G. Jung, the bonding element between psyche and matter is number, that is, the

---

[8] [See J. Gary Sparks, *At the Heart of Matter: Synchronicity and Jung's Spiritual Testament,* for commentary on von Franz's role, together with that of the physicist Wolfgang Pauli and Jung, in the explication of synchronous, acausal events connecting psyche and matter.—Ed.]

archetype of order. Dr. von Franz took on the task of elucidating the role of number in connection with synchronicity. Her premise states that there is an archetype behind every synchronistic event, bearing in mind that the archetype is not the cause of the synchronicity itself. A synchronistic event occurs at an unpredictable moment in time when psyche (which in its deepest layers is not bound to time) and matter (which is linked to the world of time) unite in a non-causal way. Her extensive knowledge in both physics and depth psychology allowed Dr. von Franz to comment on the fact that a common meaning, which cannot be foreseen, is the element always linked to the sporadic conjunction of psychic and physical events.

In 1993, Dr. von Franz was pleased to hear that the ETH, the Swiss Federal Institute of Technology in Zürich, together with the C.G. Jung Institute in Küsnacht, had arranged a five-day meeting to discuss "The Irrational in Natural Science: Wolfgang Pauli's Encounter with the Spirit of Nature." The colloquy focused on the question of how the irrational influences the work of natural scientists, the interpretation of their results, and their concepts of nature. By using the term "the irrational," von Franz remarked that scientists avoid speaking of "the unconscious." The latter, she stated, can neither be expressed through the "irrational," nor by any mathematical formula or concept, as for instance the enigmatic "Ring i." The tendency to try to control the unconscious, Dr. von Franz emphasized, is highly questionable because it aims at imprisoning the spirit of nature.

As von Franz saw it, should natural scientists come to accept the reality of the unconscious and its implications, the fateful question will be whether they will also accept the moral and ethical consequences of their endorsement. Psychologically speaking, the conflict appears to be between the prestige-addicted worldly anima versus Sophia, the anima of divine wisdom, and the pretentious worldly animus versus the animus as the spirit of truth.

In *Psychotherapy* (1993), Marie-Louise von Franz deals with many aspects of the psychotherapeutic and analytic processes. She gives practical advice based on her life-long clinical experience, and reveals some of the pitfalls lying in wait for psychotherapists. In this connection, von Franz noted as a serious problem that Jungian authors, taking pride in becoming professional in writing on Jungian psychology, too often tend to forget that the basic ideas they expound are not their own.

Intensive research stands behind her book *On Dreams & Death* (1998), in which Dr. von Franz confronts the question of the nature of death and the afterlife. To investigate this mystery, she turns primarily to dreams. According to the material she gathered, she concluded that the process of individuation does not stop at death but continues beyond the cessation of rational consciousness. Preparing for her own death, Marie-Louise von Franz made a conscious decision to endure her illness (Parkinson's disease) with a minimum of medication in order to confront, with incomparable courage and lucidity, a slow and painful dying process, thereby allowing it to last as long as the unconscious wished. The difficulty, she explained, is learning to surrender and suffer all that the dying process entails, not trying to escape it but simply accepting that there is a purpose behind it.

One evening, following an urge to tidy up her correspondence but without much thought about what she was doing, she threw away letters from a very dear friend who had died. That night she had a dream that informed her of how very pleased the unconscious was with her act. "You see," she said, "if we destroy something in this world, the other world reacts to it. But we need dreams to believe this."

Conclusion

Taking into consideration her monumental work, the fine quality and depth of her feelings, the witty humor with which she wrote in uncomplicated language, as well as her extraordinary intelligence and unsurpassable spirit, one might be tempted to think of Marie-Louise von Franz as an incarnation of Athena, born from the head of Zeus. However, Dr. von Franz was by no means the father-devoted goddess who, according to some authors, aimed at triumphing over the matriarchal sow goddess. On the contrary, her writings are living proof of her dedication to the feminine and its redemption in our time. Her interpretations of fairy tales, as well as *A Psychological Interpretation of the Golden Ass of Apuleius* (1992), give rich insight into this subject. And one of her favorite books, *The Cat: A Tale of Feminine Redemption,* has been let out of the bag (1999)! This work elaborates on the thought that a profound transformation, coinciding with the zodiacal change of our era, is about to take place through the mediation of the feminine. In Marie-Louise von Franz's view, the feminine principle of Eros will unite insight and understanding and heal the sufferings caused by an overly one-sided patriarchal outlook on life.

Acknowledgments

I would like to thank Alison Kappes for her invaluable help in reviewing this text, as well as D. Gyalistras and W. Odajnk for many helpful suggestions.

Marie-Louise von Franz at her Bollingen tower (about 1994).

Marie-Louise von Franz
The Classic Jungian

James A. Hall

My Dawning Consciousness of Jung

I first became aware of Jung in graduate school. I was enrolled as an English student and had accumulated enough credits for an M.A. in English while I was still an undergraduate. I spent the year working on a thesis (short stories), editing the *Texas Ranger* (the University of Texas humor magazine), and taking journalism courses, hoping to make myself marketable. A year later I decided to go to medical school. I did not definitely choose to specialize in psychiatry until my junior year. Certain experiences following the birth of my first child, a daughter, awakened affects in me that were connected with the birth of my only sibling, my sister, when I was three. These experiences, which included a delusion of having cancer, convinced me of the reality of the unconscious and were the proximal reason I chose to specialize in psychiatry. It took consultations with three different specialists to convince me that I was not dying.

I did not begin to read Jung until the end of my junior year in medical school when I took a trip alone to look over psychiatric residencies recommended to me by my chief. Finding myself stuck for a weekend in Chapel Hill, North Carolina, between an appointment at Duke and the University of North Carolina, I went to a bookstore to buy some reading. One of the books I found was Jolande Jacobi's *Complex/Archetype/ Symbol,* with selections from Jung's writings. They spoke to me. It was the first time I had read anything that described life as I had actually experienced it. I decided that if the opportunity ever arose, I would consult a Jungian analyst.

I chose the residency at Duke and was accepted there. During my second year, I heard that Dieter Baumann, Jung's grandson and the only psychiatrist in the Jung family, was touring the United States. I had met his brother Adrian in Dallas while he was at Neiman-Marcus studying merchandising for Bally shoes. I wrote to Dieter and asked him to visit us in Durham and see J.B. Rhine's famous Parapsychology Lab and the Duke psychiatry department. To my great joy, he accepted. He was the first live Jungian analyst I had met. One of the activities to which I introduced him was Psychosomatic Grand Rounds at Duke Hospital.

With a group of residents and one of the staff Dieter did a bedside interview of a patient, an elderly woman. He first explored the issues that any competent psychiatrist would, but then continued further, asking about her dreams. In our discussion of the case later, he convincingly linked the content of her dreams to her symptoms.

I was immensely impressed and decided to become a Jungian analyst. For the first time I had seen Jung's system as very practical and not just an intellectual pursuit. Although I did not see how it would be possible, I decided to become a Jungian analyst as well as a psychiatrist. Before Dieter left I told him of my decision. He advised me to try to analyze with either of two women who had worked closely with Jung himself—Rivkah Schärf Kluger in Los Angeles or Marie-Louise von Franz in Zürich. Eventually I was able to work with both, Rivkah in Los Angeles and Zürich and von Franz during my time at the original Jung Institute on *Gemeindestrasse* in Zürich.

Classical Jungian Analysis with von Franz: Crisis and the "Non-Empathic" Response

I analyzed simultaneously with Dieter Baumann and von Franz. Naively, I expected my thinking function to be developed by the man, my feeling function to be developed by the woman. What happened was exactly the reverse. Dieter seldom finished with a dream in one session, viewing it from many angles, squeezing out the last drop of feeling nuance. With von Franz, however, it was as if I opened her head and poured in two weeks' worth of dreams, which came back through her mouth immediately amplified and articulated with one another around an ongoing theme. I often joked that von Franz had a chrome-plated intuitive function.

In my analysis with von Franz occurred the most healing (and also dangerous) event of my work with four different analysts. It was a cold, drab day. I had run my basket of dreams through von Franz's chrome-plated hopper and was satisfied with the results. But a full quarter of my precious hour remained. I decided to tell von Franz of a spontaneous imaginal experience a few days before. While walking to the nearby grocery I had reached up to scratch my forehead when an inner male voice said distinctly, "Don't scratch the skin because it won't heal." Von Franz paused, then asked, "May I speak frankly?" I assented. She then said, "You *are* just dead!" I was devastated. If this woman, whom I felt had understood me better than anyone else in my life, judged me to be "just dead," I might as well give up trying to become an analyst and leave Zürich.

While I sat, disheartened and silent, an unusual thing

happened. Nibby, von Franz's English bulldog, left his usual spot by the stove and ambled toward me. Usually the only notice he paid me was to try to chew on my hat when I left it unguarded. This time, however, he licked my hand. Did he sense how devastated I felt? I thought to myself, "You are von Franz's dissociated feeling function, aren't you, as her familiar spirit?"

In the two weeks until my next hour with von Franz I worked unceasingly. The whole direction of my future life depended on whether I chose to stay in Zürich or end my training. Furiously I followed my dreams, did active imagination, cast *I Ching* oracles—everything. An active imagination sequence led to a lysis. In active imagination I consulted an inner figure, Manjusri, who had consistently given me good advice. Manjusri was based on a small wooden Japanese figure that had been a present from my friend Carr. My first experience of active imagination had occurred while trying to visualize this figure. Manjusri is the bodhisattva of infinite wisdom and in Tibet he appears as Yamantaka, the ferocious "destroyer of death." In one hand he holds a sword, in the other a cintomani, a jewel from the bottom of the sea.

In my active imagination, I explained to this figure my experience with von Franz and asked what I should say to her. To my surprise he handed me his sword and said, "Don't say anything to von Franz, kill her!" Now this advice constellated a problem for me. I had believed that one should not do anything in active imagination one would not do in reality, lest the active imagination lose tension and become mere fantasy. Since I would not *really* murder von Franz, therefore, I should not do it in active imagination; yet the figure of Manjusri had always given good advice. I finally resolved my quandary by pursuing von Franz with the sword *as if* to kill her, holding in suspense a final decision. The moment I began the pursuit of the figure of von Franz, she changed into an eagle. I did not wish to kill an eagle, but it was less prohibited than killing a human being. The active imagination developed further.

When my next appointment with von Franz arrived, it didn't matter at all what she thought because I knew what I thought of myself. Certainly, I was *not* dead. When I told von Franz about my conflict and its resolution, she laughingly said, "An eagle, eh? That's my animus. You can kill *that.*" This, the most impressive experience that happened to me in analysis, would today be classified as a "non-empathic" response by von Franz to me, something that as easily might have killed me as cured me—like the alchemical *tincture,* either a panacea or a deadly poison, depending on one's attitude. It was pure von Franz, perhaps possible only during what I call the classic period of Jungian analysis in Zürich. At the conclusion of this paper I will propose criteria for this period, for which von Franz is, to my mind, the outstanding representative.

External Structures/Intrapsychic Structures

My second most impressive analytic experience also occurred with von Franz. Somehow, I found myself having difficulties with three relationships that were important to me—one with Bill Walker, who later became my closest friend. Another was with Franz Riklin, then president of the Zürich Jung Institute. Since I was a common factor in all three relationships, I naturally assumed that *I* was the cause of the problem, but I had no idea as to *how.* Even my dreams gave no help. When I explained the situation to von Franz, instead of directly dealing with the situation she suggested that I paint the silver cross inlaid with turquoise that I always wore on a silver chain around my neck. Her suggestion related back to my first attempt at active imagination using the figure of Manjusri. In that experience, Manjusri had suddenly come alive, flipped horizontally the jewel in his left hand, sliced it open with his sword and out came the turquoise and silver cross: a Maltese cross of silver inlaid with turquoise. Each arm had a flat truncated wedge of turquoise. Interior to the four arms, a ring of eight small spheres of turquoise circled a large central oval turquoise.

It all vanished as quickly as it had come. Needless to say I was impressed, so impressed that I had a jeweler friend craft it. In retrospect, I suppose it was more a *vision* than what I would now call active imagination. On the way home from my session I went by the Niederdorf and bought paints and canvas. As I painted the cross, however, a strange thing happened: the outer four stones wanted to rotate counterclockwise, the eight small stones clockwise, and the central stone from left to right about a vertical axis. To paint all this was, of course, physically impossible, but I duly indicated the rotation in the painting, which I still have. When I judged that my painting was finished I left it to dry and went to bed. But I could not sleep. Something about the painting was unfinished. About 2:30 a.m. I arose, and with my pocketknife I punched a tiny hole in the center of the central stone. Now the painting seemed complete. I went to bed and slept soundly until morning.

But what did it all mean? What did it have to do with my simultaneous conflict with three relationships? Since I had come to consider counterclockwise rotation to signify movement toward the unconscious, I decided it might mean to be more unconscious and spontaneous in my outer relations. So for three days I did just that, reacting spontaneously without hesitation or reflection. My three troubled relationships smoothed out. Apparently I *had* been the cause of the difficulties, for they disappeared with my change of attitude. I reported this to von Franz but alas I do not recall her response.

Transference/Countertransference (T/C)

Doubtless I had transference feelings for von Franz. Once for a full week I even had strong sexual feelings for her. This surprised me, as I felt no conscious sexual attraction. My classic memory of von Franz is of her sitting in her consulting room chain-smoking, wearing a baggy tweed skirt, knees akimbo like a truck driver.

Within a week the sexual feelings evaporated, to be briefly replaced by a feeling that she was a waif in need of protection. For a few days I even considered adding her to my hospitalization insurance.

Dream Analysis

I once took von Franz a dream that I was afraid might mean I had undiagnosed cancer. In the dream I found gold coins growing like flat warts on my thigh. There was a cone of gold, too, growing in my knee. I could remove it to observe the structure of the joint. I could think of nothing other than inorganic metal growing where flesh ought to be. Without a word von Franz began looking through her extensive library. As the minutes passed I remembered Rivkah Kluger telling me how she had felt waiting for Jung to find just the right amplification for her dream while her precious hour ticked away.

Finally von Franz found the right book. She put in my hands R.B. Onian's *Origins of European Thought* opened to the section "Birth from the Knee." What I read relieved all my anxiety about cancer. Later, the same dream yielded many alchemical parallels through active imagination.

The Future of Jungian Analysis

Years later I visited von Franz with Bill Walker. She and Barbara Hannah were vacationing at a spa, Bad Regaz. I asked von Franz about what she saw as the future of Jungian psychology over the next few decades because it seemed to be splintering in so many directions. She thought for a moment then said, "It will be like early Taoism—a few masters but many street magicians." At lunch I could see in von Franz early signs of the Parkinsonism that progressively incapacitated her. On another visit I was impressed that von Franz remembered in detail a dream from my analysis over two decades before. Emboldened, I asked her to comment on a dream I had had the year before. It had disturbed me considerably, but when my mother died suddenly a few months later I believed it had been a foreshadowing to prepare me for that shock.

I dreamed I was in "Death's house" sitting across from him at his table. He was an older man in a business suit, kind and gentlemanly in manner. As he rose to leave he gestured toward a dark descending stairway to my right. "If you wish, I'll show you what's downstairs," he said, adding, "but you won't like it." Although Death had said nothing particularly threatening, I was near panic when he left the room. There were two doors between the room I was in and the outside. Were they locked? I found both open. I bounded out of the house, jumped off a low cliff, and found myself floating in an inner tube in Club Lake, a small fishing lake near my hometown. Interestingly, it is unsuitable for swimming. I saw our cabin across the lake. Just then Wally, a friend since the eighth grade, and his wife arrived from my right, paddling tubes and playfully splashing water at me. Wally dunked my head under water.

I told von Franz the dream and that I thought it had foreshadowed my mother's death. Without hesitating she replied, "You should have looked downstairs!" I agreed. Later, in active imagination, I did look downstairs in Death's house and was surprised at what I found—pottery shards! For a while I took these to be shards of people's broken lives. Later I came to think of them as shards like those in the cabalistic image of the *Quipthoth,* "the world of shards," which consists of remnants of the ten broken "vessels" which were constructed to contain God's emanations but proved too weak. I associated more to Wally. He was a tragic figure, jovial on the outside yet actually deeply depressed, who progressively had withdrawn from life. Only in the three days between the two episodes of pulmonary bleeding that killed him did Wally show signs that this trend might be reversing.

On one visit I asked von Franz her conclusion on survival after death. I had just finished reading her book *On Dreams & Death: A Jungian Interpretation.* She answered immediately, "When I die I'll know—or I won't know and it won't matter." She was a true empiricist, like Jung himself.

Trust in the Unconscious

Von Franz trusted the unconscious more than anyone I have known. Once she told me that after she finished writing *Number and Time,* which covers integers 1-4, she had a series of dreams that suggested she abandon further work on higher numbers. So she threw away her notes. I often wonder about Jung's well-known views of the number 4. Why does the alchemical Axiom of Maria only deal with the numbers 1, 2, 3 and 4, and 4=1;[9] why are there 4 worlds in the *Kabbalah;* why

---

[9] [The Axiom reads: "One becomes two, two becomes three, and out of the third comes the one as the fourth." *(Psychology and Alchemy,* CW 12, par. 26); see also *Jung Uncorked,* Book One, p. 51)—Ed.]

4 rows in the Pythagorean tetractys? Once when von Franz dreamed of a burning house, she took the image at first subjectively, wondering if her psychic "house" suffered from an excess of unconfined libido. But when she went on a previously arranged visit to friends and found that their house had burned down about the time of the dream, she considered the dream to be objective and not about herself.

Von Franz was always mindful of her own mental hygiene. She found herself spending excessive time thinking of a garage she wanted to build at *Lindenbergstrasse* 15, the hillside home she shared with Barbara Hannah in Küsnacht. Rather than cluttering up her mind with schemes of how to afford the expensive garage, she simply decided to put her excess money in a small box for a reasonable period of time. If she accumulated enough to build the garage, she would; if not, she would forget it. (It never was built.)

Jung Stories

Occasionally von Franz told me stories of Jung. She once said that Jung often had intellectual insights that later he had to experience in his own life. I have found this true in my own experience. One day we were talking of the possibility of reincarnation. Von Franz casually dropped a bombshell. After the death of Toni Wolff, Jung's long-time paramour, she said he thought Toni might have been reincarnated as a young girl who lived near Zürich. For several years he had carefully followed the girl's development, even speculating as to *why* Toni would need to reincarnate. But I find only one sentence in his autobiography that might refer to this preoccupation,[10] although there are several paragraphs that consider the

[10] *Memories, Dreams, Reflections,* p. 319.

possibility of survival after death.

Only slowly has it dawned on me that what I experienced with von Franz was not what most people nowadays mean by "Jungian analysis." However, it was Jungian analysis at a particular time and place by those who had known Jung himself. In addition to von Franz, I think of Barbara Hannah, Dieter Baumann, Jolande Jacobi, H.K. Fiertz, Mary Brinner, C.A. Meier, Rivkah Kluger, Aniela Jaffé and Liliane Frey-Rohn, and Edward F. Edinger among others. I call this the Classic Period, which followed just after Jung.

I think T.S. Eliot was correct: what is true is true only for one time and for one place, as though components that define a period may again be emphasized (and modified by) another time, place and context—just as in the *I Ching* the trigram Ch'ien, heaven, is a component of many hexagrams, each with a unique meaning.

Classic Jungian Analysis

I once made a list of ten characteristics that I feel distinguish this time period. Barbara Davies showed an earlier version of this list containing points 1-7 to von Franz, who remarked, "That about covers it." Here are my ten points:

1. The centrality of the dream, as revelatory of the Self.
   a. Emphasis on amplification.
   b. Frequent use of active imagination.

2. The Self, or Archetypal Self, seen as unifying "opposites" and as essentially positive.

3. Seeing the ego as a part of the Self, the "vicar of the Self in consciousness," so to speak.

4. A Socratic methodology—a dialogue drawing material

primarily from the client, supplemented by the analyst's amplifications with historical and mythological motifs.

5. Emphasis on dreams and active imagination rather than on the transference/countertransference (T/CT), with a tendency to see the analyst and analysand as allies in dealing with the analysand's unconscious.

corollary l: Friendship is a natural terminus of analysis.
corollary 2: If anything significant is to happen the analyst, too, must be involved in the process.

6. An emphasis on the responsibility of each person for his/her own individuation process.

7. "High carelessness" (free-wheeling) in the use of the intuitive function, but *only after* the sensation function has gathered as much data as possible *from the dreamer.*

8. The goal of analysis is seen as growth or "individuation" rather than cure.

9. A tendency to see any structures given focal attention as reflecting, through projection, their gestalt and analogous structure of intrapsychic contents. Thus, psychological thinking is metaphorical, involving an ability to recognize a similarity between outer (objective) and inner (subjective) patterns.

l0. Considering the inner world to be of equal weight or value as the external world and a belief that both worlds are finally one *(unus mundus).* With each dream a decision must be made whether to interpret it objectively, subjectively, or both.

For me, Marie-Louise von Franz will always be the classic Jungian. All of us classic Jungians are now faced with the struggle to be masters or to be analyzed by masters, and to let the street magicians play to the crowd.

Marie-Louise von Franz in her Küsnacht study room (1994).

The Lifestyle of Marie-Louise von Franz An Interview with Barbara Davies and James A. Hall

Robert S. Henderson

Barbara Davies, Ph.D., is a Jungian therapist with a private practice in Zürich. She worked intensively with and for Dr. von Franz for over twelve years. Presently she is working on a new German translation of von Franz's *Interpretation of Fairy Tales*. Barbara grew up in Geneva and received her doctorate in psychology from the University of Zürich. She gives seminars in Zürich, throughout Europe and Australia. She is the mother of Richard who is married to Susi, and grandmother of two-year-old Maceo.

James A. Hall, M.D., is a retired Jungian analyst/psychiatrist/poet in Dallas. He is a graduate of the University of Texas, Southwestern Medical School, and the C.G. Jung Institute in Zürich. He is the author of seven works on Jungian psychology, including *Jungian Dream Interpretation: A Handbook of Theory and Practice* (Inner City Books, 1983) and *Hypnosis: A Jungian Perspective* (Guilford Press, 1989). In 1992 he was disabled by a brainstem stroke, which left him with locked-in syndrome, quadriplegic and mute, but with normal sensorium and intellect. The story of his post-stroke struggle to communicate is told in *Locked in to Life* (TeaRoad), written with Patton Howell. Using a splint attached to his right index finger, typing one letter at a time, he uses his laptop computer to maintain a wide network of friendships, participate in professional organizations, and contribute to the literature of Jungian psychology. He and his wife, Suzanne, have been together fifty years. They have two daughters and a grandson.

Robert Henderson (RH): What are a couple of your favorite stories about Dr. von Franz?

Barbara Davies (BD): Dr. von Franz and I often talked about death. One morning she and I spoke about letters that had been written by her or by me to people we loved but who, in the meantime, had died. We debated the question as to whether or not it was right to destroy these letters as well as when it was time to do so. Dr. von Franz explained to me that if we destroy something in this world the other world reacts to it. "But we need dreams to believe this," she added.

We also talked about the fact that we know too little about the time of our death. We thought the post between the Beyond and here should be improved. She complained about not being better informed about when her time to go would be. So I told her we could try writing a registered letter and send it by tachions! Tears of laughter rolled down![11]

James Hall (JH): Here are two examples of her English bulldog, Nibby, helping her in her work. In both examples Nibby acts in lieu of von Franz's inferior feeling. (This was also true of Jung himself. He tells of having conversations with his anima to learn his feelings.[12] Later in life he had direct awareness of them.)

The first example occurred during one of my regular sessions with von Franz. She interpreted all my recent dreams in her rapid machine-gun style, amplifying and relating them to

---

[11] Tachions are supposed to be particles traveling faster than light. "Serious" theoretical physicists will of course have nothing to do with them. At the time Marlus and I were talking about these particles, tachions were spoken of occasionally, but of course just lightly and only as a possibility. One day, who knows, we may hear that these particles can be detected!

[12] *Memories, Dreams, Reflections,* pp. 186ff.

my individuation process. Many minutes of my precious hour remained. What to talk about? Suddenly I recalled a spontaneous imaginal experience a few days before: I reached up to scratch my forehead when an authoritative Inner Voice said, "Don't break the skin—it won't heal." "May I speak frankly?" she asked.

"Of course."

"You *are* just dead!"

I was shattered. If this woman, whom I thought understood me better than anyone else, thought of me as "just dead," perhaps I should leave Zürich and give up analytic training.

At that very moment Nibby left his usual spot by the stove and ambled toward me. Usually the only notice he paid me was to try to chew on my hat when I left it unguarded. This time, however, he licked my hand. Did he sense how devastated I felt? Did he want to comfort me, to reassure me that "all will be well; all manner of things will be well"?

I thought to myself, "Nibby, you are von Franz's dissociated feeling function, aren't you—her familiar spirit?"

In the two weeks until my next appointment I worked diligently on my dreams and active imaginations. My future was at stake. I *must* find my own position about myself. The lysis came in an active imagination of Manjusri, bodhisattva of infinite wisdom. He always gave me good advice. I told him my problem, and then asked, "What should I *say* to von Franz?"

"Say nothing," he replied, offering me his unsheathed sword. "Take my sword and kill her."

Now this was a real crisis! I believed one should not do anything in active imagination that one would not do if it were an actual situation. To do so would change the active imagination into a mere fantasy. In a fantasy, "anything goes" because "nothing counts." My conflict: I would not actually kill von Franz but Manjusri had always given me good advice. Finally I pursued her *as if* to kill her, postponing a decision to actually do so. The moment I began the pursuit, von Franz changed into an eagle. I did not wish to kill an eagle, but it was less prohibited than killing a human being.

The active imagination developed further, and when my next appointment with von Franz arrived, it didn't matter at all what she thought because I knew what I thought of myself. *I* knew that I was alive—and becoming more so. When I told her my active imagination she said it was the best thing that happened during my analysis with her.

But it could have been the worst had I reacted differently. It could have been the end of everything—my analysis, my training, my involvement with the Classic Jungian Tradition and membership in the International Association.

When I told von Franz about my conflict and its resolution, she laughingly said, "An eagle, eh? That's my animus. You can kill *that!*"

She then told me how Nibby had helped when an elderly female Freudian asked for analysis, first saying she just wanted to compare the Jungian and Freudian theories.

Von Franz was already thinking of reasons to decline an analysis motivated purely by intellectual curiosity. Suddenly Nibby jumped in the woman's lap. It startled her. She began to cry and tell the *real* reason she sought a Jungian analysis—a seemingly intractable life problem. On that basis von Franz accepted her for analysis.

(RH): Barbara, how did you meet Dr. von Franz?

(BD): The first time I met Marie-Louise von Franz and Barbara Hannah was at an invitation to have tea with them in Küsnacht.

My analyst at that time was a friend of the ladies and she had arranged the meeting. The motive behind our having tea was the possibility of my having a few hours of analysis with Miss Hannah. I was terribly intimidated by the two ladies and sat there as stiff as a pole putting on my best and most unnatural good manners which, later on, I realized was the very thing I needn't and shouldn't have done.

The next time I met von Franz was for a short analysis. I had had a dream that fascinated me and which I thought indicated I should study at the Jung Institute. However, at that time I didn't have the required certificate to allow me to enter the Institute. Secretly I believed von Franz would put in a good word for me. Instead she cut the hour short, accompanied me to the door and bluntly told me to go back to school and start studying for the university entrance certificate. Crush, bang! Even the weather hated me. Heavy clouds were hanging over Küsnacht and cold rain added to my depression.

Some years later I had another meeting with Barbara Hannah for dream analysis. She predicted the one thing I didn't want to hear: studying for the university entrance would feel like a hundred exams.

Years later my analyst told me von Franz was looking for someone to help with her private correspondence and with a book on Arabic alchemy. I had been suggested. Marie-Louise had Parkinson's disease and it had become increasingly difficult for her to write. The reason I was chosen for this work was mainly due to a dream I had had on Arabic alchemy and probably also because I felt easy in three languages.

The very first time I was to work for her it had been decided I would meet her at her tower on the top of a little hill in the woods of Bollingen. (I never made it that day and later sent her a telegram telling her I had become lost.) For some unknown reason I drove down to the lake in Bollingen. Still not knowing where I was, I knocked at the door of a beautiful private house where I hoped people would tell me how to find Dr. von Franz. That is how, for the first time, I came to Jung's tower.

Working for Marie-Louise was both scary and an enormous enrichment. She loved animals and it turned out that she cared a lot for my smart little Yorkshire terrier, Pie-Pie, who fell head over heels in love with Marlus's dog, Laura. The latter would wait in the dining room on a big green leather armchair for Pie-Pie to reach up to her and kiss her nose. That was the ritual. Marlus told me to keep Pie-Pie with me as an assistant during analytic sessions. Indeed, over the years Pie-Pie's reactions have proved to be infallible.

I loved the mornings when Marie-Louise was waiting for me, smoking a cigarette. Her smoking before commencing our work was a sign of a relaxed morning ahead. Often she would first tell me the latest jokes she had heard and only then did we start work. About half the time was spent attending to her private letters, the other half on her creative work. I loved having to go to the central library in Zürich to do research or bring back books. Marie-Louise's hunger for books was insatiable. When she prepared to go for her annual two months' vacation to Bollingen, innumerable paper shopping bags had to be filled with books. Whenever I had read a book which she hadn't read but which related to her interests and to her work, I was instructed to buy it for her and she eagerly waited to have it in her own hands.

Most precious were our discussions during and after work. I always tried to memorize them and write them down.

The way she paid my wages was as unconventional as the way she taught me to keep track of which publishers had finally paid her. I took my salary out of a moneybox that she kept above the fireplace. Marie-Louise could be ferocious and terrible yet immensely compassionate, forgiving, and understanding of one's weaknesses. I often thought her patience with me was about to run out. It never did. On the contrary: she endured my inferior function with great composure and we shared many laughs about it.

She also shared with me many memories of her life. Our relationship grew deeper over the years. I cannot find the right words to describe the extraordinary relationship I was permitted to experience with a lady whose greatness of spirit and true humility surpasses anything I have come across so far.

(RH): In addition to her writing and analytical work, how did she like to spend her energy and time?

(BD): Reading was her main occupation when she was not working. Marie-Louise absolutely loved books and bought many. She once told a friend of mine that she was "drowning in books" and added, "What a glorious way to die!" Besides reading, when she had time, she occasionally enjoyed seeing visitors and having tea with them. She loved jokes and could tell a joke with excellent timing. It has to be mentioned that, in general, Marie-Louise was reluctant to speak of her private life.

(JH): She worked in her garden. When Fraser Boa was interviewing her for *The Way of the Dream* film series, her fingernails were often grimy. Between filming sessions she was working in her garden.

(RH): What are some of the memories you have of her private life?

(JH): I was, of course very interested in her private life—not only because she was my analyst and friend. Also because she lived her life by her understanding of basic Jungian (universal?) principles. Thus von Franz's life, as much as her writings, lectures and her one film series, exemplifies the Classic Jungian Tradition.

She once told me she received invitations to lecture from many parts of the world. She was tempted to accept them but did not want to travel while her dog Nibby was alive. Nibby needed her. This is only one example of von Franz's loyalty, even to her dog.

For many years she shared a house at *Lindenbergstrasse* 15 in Küsnacht with Barbara Hannah, another respected analyst. Once Barbara fell ill in a place some distance from Zürich. When von Franz went to visit Barbara burst into tears. After all their years together she was still surprised that von Franz cared enough about her to visit her when she was ill.

I found von Franz very loyal to the individuation process in herself or others, which could make her seem cold and insensitive from the point of view of one's currently dominant ego-image, what I call "doegi" for short.

Although von Franz rarely spoke of her private life, I do not think she was reticent to do so or guarded in any way. Rather she seemed to think her private life of little interest to herself or others. Like Jung himself she always seemed focused on the archetypal process, and neither wrote of their relationships.

(RH): What are some of the things you learned from Marie-Louise that you have never forgotten?

(BD): Unforgettable in my life is the way I experienced her absolute devotion regarding her dreams and her consultation of the *I Ching* when she was in doubt. All her dreams were written into a red book, which she asked to be burned at her death.

Of all the things she taught me, the deepest was how to face death and how to endure a slow and long dying process.

From her I also learned not to be afraid to look at who may betray you one day and to take it as a matter of fact.

She taught me how to stick to my work no matter what. This I learned the day I told her that I wasn't cut out for the work of an analyst, that it was simply too much for me. She looked at me critically and said: "*le vin est tiré, il faut le boire,*" which means, "You opened the bottle of wine, now drink it!"

(JH): I learned from both her teaching and from the example of her own life. I learned to look at each dream from two view-points, first subjective then objective. I learned the primacy of dreams in both analysis and individuation.

I learned the value of archetypal amplification. I learned the value of active imagination. I learned the value of enactments, expressive arts, notably painting my dream images and fantasies. By her own example she taught me not to worry so much about money (a lesson I'm still learning) and to notice things happening, perhaps synchronistic allies, in emotional moments—for example, the behavior of her dog. I was blessed by having great teachers, and the greatest was von Franz.

(RH): Barbara, I suspect a lot of what she taught you about facing death and enduring the dying process came from what Marie-Louise von Franz shared with you and also how you saw her deal with her own death. What are some of the things you learned about this profound aspect of life?

(BD): While bearing the clash of the opposites within herself and struggling with her own imminent death, von Franz taught me a profound lesson about life. On the one hand, she was impatient to go, to be gone, to bring an end to the process that deals with the cadaver, as she called it. On the other hand, she was deeply committed to her ongoing process of learning which, at this final stage, she felt was the process of learning "how to become spirit," of learning to completely let go of the outer world in favor of the experience ahead.

(RH): Like Jung, Dr. von Franz had a summer place at Bollingen on Lake Zürich. What was it like?

(BD): Whereas Jung built a round tower by the lake of Zürich, Marie-Louise had a square tower built on top of a hill. Her hermitage was situated next to a small natural pond at the edge of the woods that surrounded her property.

(JH): Rustic and primitive—like Jung's tower. Once she met me at the Bollingen station and drove me there. Another time I went by car from Zürich and had difficulty finding it.

Marie-Louise von Franz's tower at Bollingen.

Marie-Louise von Franz with her bulldog Nibby (1986).

On Love, Maturity and Happiness
An Interview with Marie-Louise von Franz, Jung's foremost pupil[13]

Joan Juliet Buck

It is perhaps von Franz's extreme modesty and strict respect for the laws of reality that have made her books and lectures not only popular in Jungian circles, but inspiring for writers. Her book on *The Problem of the Puer Aeternus,* which describes the neurosis of a person who cannot grow up, commit, or get to work, applies perfectly to those who believe creativity itself is art. Among the symptoms she describes are "a terrific fear of being pinned down, of entering time and space completely, and of being the specific human being that one is." In 1983, Dan Kiley took up and simplified her ideas in *The Peter Pan Syndrome,* which became a bestseller.

"For the first half of my life, I wrote for the drawer," says Dr. von Franz, who is quick to point out that she is a doctor of classical languages, not of medicine.

She once co-authored a book on the symbolism of fairy tales with a woman named Hedwig Von Beit, who had assembled the material but found herself blocked. Von Franz wrote it, while Von Beit did the footnotes and bibliography, but the book appeared without von Franz's name. Contrast this with *The Grail Legend,* which bears the double authorship of Emma Jung and Marie-Louise von Franz. Asked how she and Jung's wife worked together, Dr. von Franz explains: "Mrs. Jung arranged with her husband that I should finish her book after her death, and it was only after

---

[13] Excerpt from *Vogue* magazine, November 1986, pp. 206ff.

she died that Jung told me about her request. So then the Jung's chauffer came and dumped an enormous mass of manuscript on my desk. I'd had no connection with it before. I've done the finishing for a lot of people. I'm that kind of person, a servant."

Dr. von Franz is now seventy-one [1986]; she lives and practices in Küsnacht, the same suburb of Zürich where Jung lived and where the Jung Institute is today. The house is small, on a steep street, and its study is dark. On the days I saw her, it was raining and the air was dense with water.

Dr. von Franz is in frail health, but steadied, sturdy. She has extraordinarily luminous eyes, a straight long nose, a soft mouth, and her hair is carefully dressed. Her skin is transparent, and the extreme nobility of her features suggests a universe of uncertain energies beneath the skin. The bookshelves sag under volumes in Latin, German, Greek and English. Her spoken English is easy, idiomatic; she says she learned it in her practice from her Anglo-Saxon patients, starting with an FBI man. A large and unruly bulldog, female, yowls to punctuate von Franz's words.

Her first three books were followed by a series of lectures on the interpretation of fairy tales, which made her famous. Her other books take a Jungian approach to mathematics *(Number and Time),* to coincidence *(On Divination and Synchronicity),* and to alchemy *(Alchemy: An Introduction to the Symbolism and the Psychology, Alchemical Active Imagination* and *Aurora Consurgens).* Her book *Projection and Re-Collection* is a brilliant work on illusion and reality, as much in psychology and religion as in relationships. Her approach to love deals honestly with it as a problem instead of as a solution. "Whoever cannot surrender to this experience has never lived," she says, "whoever founders in it has understood nothing."

Projection and Re-Collection is a central book; it addresses an issue at the heart of psychology, religion and philosophy: What is real? "It's only since the eighteenth-century Enlighten-ment that man has begun to believe that there is only one reality, this one, the material one. In Africa, the tribes not yet influenced by missions take it for granted that there are ghosts, and in the Middle Ages it was accepted that there were ghosts and uncanny effects, which were called God or the Devil. There is an ordinary collective world where one thinks things are real, and that is very much influenced by the *Zeitgeist,* the spirit of the times; then there is the unknown, the surprising, the frightening, which we call the unconscious."

In the first chapter, she quotes Jung on the phenomenon of projection: "Just as we tend to assume the world is as we see it, we naively suppose that people are as we imagine them to be. In this way everyone creates for himself a series of more or less imaginary relationships based essentially on projection." The task of dissolving these imaginary relationships is not easy. "It's a question," she says, "of either living in illusion, in which case you don't feel you are living a true life, or facing reality as it is, and it is horrible and dangerous. There is a kind of kindergarten mentality that Christianity bred in people. If you behave well, you will go to Paradise. There is a Good Shepherd on top who looks after you and sees that nothing goes wrong if you don't make a mistake. That's an infantile and stupid image of God, who is dual, a wonderful and a terrible thing.

"If one digs deep enough, one comes to the Indian concept of Maya, that the whole outer world is a kind of staged thing, staged by your own unconscious. It is a wisdom that throws you out of your naïve relationship with the world, a deathbed realization, and something that helps you more to die than to live. If this realization had an effect on people, it would be to make them more responsible for their reality. They would cease believing their own projections, they would not think they are the victims of their enemies, of the wrong government and so on. They'd take full responsibility for their fate. It is a realization that belongs to the second half of life, and if you come to it, then you empty the glass of wine to the last drop while knowing that you can do without it too."

Von Franz defines happiness as "functioning meaningfully." As she explains, "People have different levels of depth. There are people who are like corks and swim on the surface of the water, and some have more lead, which pulls them deeper, and everybody has to live on their own level. Some people are allowed childish happiness. I used to envy them a bit when I was younger, when I saw people just sitting on a beach and enjoying the sunshine and a flirtation, while I sat there asking myself, 'What's the meaning of life? What was I born for?' *Happy* is such an ambiguous word."

For Jung, the unconscious is an objective fact, beyond the limits of personal experience. "Freud was necessary for a liberation of the sexual prejudices of the nineteenth century," von Franz says. "Jung did not translate to the public because he was too difficult, too far ahead. He threatened rationalism. People are afraid of the unconscious and deny its reality. You can explain the unconscious away as nothing but repressed incestuous sex, and then you have it in your pocket. But maybe you have to admit there is a mysterious power with which you have to come to terms. . . ."

The danger in simplifying Jung's ideas leads to an automatic sighting of symbols and a tendency to see things as *repre-senting* rather than simply *being*. And in the path toward "individuation" (the Jungian term for the reconciling of opposites, the attainment of a functioning, harmonious person-ality), things are neither as simple nor as direct as one might wish. If Freudian analysts personally tend to err in their behavior toward the didactic, Jungians can appear eccentric. At one point, Dr. von Franz says: "I had a criminal patient the other day, and I had with him the most profound conversation I have ever had about God."

"You need to have a problem," she says, "what Jung called the unredeemed fourth function"—and what others would merely call the weak spot, the flaw, the vices. "Your inferior function [i.e., the less developed part of your personality] always involves you in new problems and makes the flow of life continue. It's only in death that problems stop. Either you repeat the same experiences and never find the meaning—and then nothing results—or you don't venture into getting involved, and you haven't lived. So you have to live and learn from it. If you change, everything around you changes. Your whole experience of reality changes. Reality is nothing objective; it is how you experience it."

Her own experience seems to have been circumscribed by self-doubt and modesty, and exalted through analysis with Jung and later work with him. "I'd had an unhappy childhood," she says, "and had made up my mind that the world was a place without love, without charity, without honesty. When I came into contact with Jung's warmth and understanding, it was like a block of ice thawing, and I dissolved into tears, which annoyed Jung, who hated to see a lady cry."

Her father was an Austrian officer, an old-fashioned monar-chist; her mother "a Voltairian materialist." As a child during the First World War, she heard two maids talking in the kitchen about battlefield atrocities. "I remember lying awake at night and saying to myself, 'Either God exists and does not stop it, in which case He is evil, or He does not exist, and that is why such things happen.' With that, I stopped saying my prayers." She became religious at eleven "in the Greek, pagan sense. I read Homer's *Odyssey,* by the sea, and I thought, 'That I can pray to, to the sea, to the sky, to the clouds, and to the mysterious powers within nature—those are the gods.' "

Her analysis with Jung developed into an exchange of views, a conversation about "inner and outer things," which changed all the time. "He aged a lot, and I grew a bit more mature; in the beginning it was a crush, a positive father transference, which is full of projection and looks like the great love but it is really a very egocentric affair, full of desires and wishes and romantic fantasies. As I grew up I was able to see him as he was, not simply as a hero figure of my own unconscious."

Each step that she took in life was decided by her unconscious, and in her story the unconscious is a constant presence, a guide and a threat, an inexorable point of reference, and also, it seems, a companion.

When her dreams urge her on, she says, "I have no choice, I have to write. The creative urge in me is so powerful that I know it would cut my throat if I didn't obey." For her, "Creativity is when there is no unconscious doubt, when the unconscious wants you to produce that image or that idea. When you are in harmony, you are the funnel through which the unconscious flows, and that is creativity."

In Jung's autobiography, *Memories, Dreams, Reflections,* he says that inner events have always had more meaning for him than outer ones; and it is the same for Dr. von Franz. In her small study, it became clear what the sacrifices are, and that they are not, in the end, sacrifices, but choices. Marie-Louise von Franz never married. "That was one of the troubles when I was young. Something conventional and collective in me wanted to get married, and my dreams were always against it. Having children was not part of my wish. I only like children when they begin to grow up and you can talk to them. Looking back, I think the reason the unconscious didn't want me to marry is that I'm not very strong physically, and it would have taken too much energy; I need twelve hours' sleep a night, and I wouldn't have written my books."

In the documentary film *Matter of Heart,* directed by Mark Whitney and written by Jungian analyst Suzanne Wagner, Dr. von Franz talks about Jung's vision of a terrible disaster that might wipe out humanity. In person, she is less dramatic: "I sometimes think the negative side, nuclear catastrophe, will prevail—the dark side of God. But one cannot live in constant anxiety; one must get on with one's own life. But when you get older, your personal life doesn't matter so much anymore; you are packing to go off, so you are slowly loosening your ties to the world. What I see—and that was the same with Jung when he got old—is that you are more anxious for humanity as a whole. The life of the planet concerns you."

She has found one thing common to all the dreams of the dying she has seen: "They all talk about a continuation of life. I have not met one dream that talks about an end." This might surprise some, and too easily confirm the beliefs of others. Coming from Marie-Louise von Franz, however, it is at once eerie, reassuring and logical—a way of continuing the dialogue with the unruly and powerful other side, the unconscious.

PART TWO
The Classic Jungian Tradition

Marie-Louise von Franz (1980).

The Classic Jungian Tradition

James A. Hall

When I was in training in the late 1960s at the original Zürich Jung Institute on *Gemeindestrasse,* the major tension in the Jungian world was between Zürich and London, England.

Zürich represented the Classic Jungian Tradition (CJT), exemplified by Jung and von Franz.

The London Jungians clustered around Michael Fordham, a pediatrician. He himself had not been analyzed by Jung. This group was influenced strongly by Melanie Klein, D.W. Winnicott and object relations theory. I call that the Classic Developmental Tradition (CDT). The Zürich and London schools are often seen as opposites that one must choose between, but personally I think they are best seen as complementary. Both are needed to maintain or restore order.

Elsewhere in the present volume I have listed attributes of the Classic Jungian Tradition. I will now flesh out that skeletal frame. Here is my complete list of characteristics that I feel distinguish the Classic time period of Jungian psychology as practiced by Marie-Louise von Franz and others during Jung's lifetime and for some years after.

l. The centrality of the dream as revealing the guiding wisdom of the Self, regulating center of the psyche.

The essence of the CJT is the activation of the transcendent function, which manifests in two stages if the tension between opposite courses of action is held long enough. First, often in a dream, a symbol arises from the unconscious. The second stage is conscious analysis, understanding, integration and application of that symbol's meaning, which effects a change in the attitude of consciousness.[14]

a. Emphasis on archetypal amplification.

In my other essay in this volume I told a dream of a gold cone growing in my knee—hard metal where flesh should be. Did I have cancer? Von Franz found the right amplification in R.B. Onian's *Origins of European Thought,* referring me to the section "Birth from the Knee." What I read relieved all my anxiety about cancer. Later, the dream yielded many alchemical parallels through active imagination.

b. Frequent use of active imagination and the two principles of projection and personification.

The most important event in my own personal analysis was in an active imagination of Manjusri, the bodhisattva of infinite wisdom. This is more fully described above (page 64). There I also give an example of von Franz analyzing a complex problem by suggesting I paint a picture of the silver and turquoise cross I always wore on a silver chain around my neck. I painted it. Within three days my viewpoint shifted and the "problem" dissolved.

The two principles of projection and personification comprise the first move of the transcendent function. Any psychic content that has no connection to ego is unconscious. When constellated (energized/activated), unconscious contents usually appear in projected form, often personified.

A repressed conflict confronts one as an outer challenge. Vicki, an attractive woman of twenty-seven, refused to see obvious problems in her marriage. She spent most lunch hours

---

[14] [For a comprehensive statement of the CJT approach to dreams see James A. Hall, *Jungian Dream Interpretation: A Handbook of Theory and Practice.*—Ed.]

at a downtown hotel in bed with a man from the office. But she avoided actual genital contact. In this bizarre context she also developed the firmly fixed delusion of a brain tumor. Several medical workups, all negative, did not impact her delusion. Indeed, there was a tumor that would end her present neurotic type of life. But it was in her *psyche,* not her brain. She hoped her problem could be solved by others while she passively submitted her body for neurosurgery and chemo- and radiation therapy. But what was really required was her active participation with enough moral courage to face her inner split *as a conflict,* rather than repressing it, causing it to manifest as a delusional brain tumor. Only then could the transcendent function appear as a symbolic solution. Finally, without discussing it with me, she signed herself into a psychiatric hospital. I lost track of her and unfortunately do not know the rest of her story.

In hospital residency we were told a story illustrating the persistence of psychotic delusions. A psychiatrist was treating a schizophrenic who had a delusion that he was dead. For six months nothing changed. Frustrated, the doctor tied a tourniquet around the man's arm, drew out 50 c.c. of red blood and squirted them dramatically against the white porcelain of a basin, saying triumphantly, "There! That *proves* you're alive!" "No, doctor," replied the schizophrenic calmly, "it only proves that corpses bleed."

2. The Self, the Archetypal Self, is seen as unifying opposites and as primarily positive.

The unification of opposites does *not* mean their average. By analogy, water, steam and ice are quite different experiences. Yet we know that steam and ice are forms of water. The unification of steam and ice is not water; it is the simultaneous presence of water, steam and ice. Any point on that continuum is free to manifest. None are repressed.

Although the Self is seen as primarily positive, the many negative aspects of life are, of course, not ignored. They are seen as compensations, warnings that one is unbalanced. In my second year of residency I fell into a relationship that in six months would lead to a conflict lasting more than two years. I dreamed I was in a small English town walking down a steep street toward the sea. At the bottom of the street I turn right into a sawdust restaurant and order their specialty—a large cone of non-melting vanilla ice cream covered with chopped fresh dates and served on a cake stand. Because dates grow on a date palm, it is called a Palm Sundae. When awake I saw at once that Palm Sundae = Palm Sunday = a triumphal entry into Jerusalem just prior to imminent crucifixion. At the time, however, I did not relate the dream to my outer life. Had I done so, the motif of non-melting ice cream might have led me to see the unreality of my situation. Did the Self, maker of my dreams, foresee the outcome of my situation and send me a whimsical warning?

Though I can *think* of a "dark side of the Self," I have seen no empirical evidence for it in the thousands of dreams I have interpreted. Dr. von Franz, with much more clinical experience, told me that she had seen only *one dream* that suggested the dream-maker, the Self, had given up on the ego. The dream was presented to her without associations or clinical data. She knew only that the dreamer was an incarcerated adult male. In his dream he is on a "cosmic swing" amid stars and suns, planets and moons. Suddenly he slips out of the swing and falls helplessly into cold and empty endless space. After von Franz commented on the bleak prognosis suggested by the dream, she was told that it was the dream of a remorseless serial killer.

3. Seeing the ego as the central complex of consciousness, but subordinate to the Self.

This truth is very hard for anyone to accept, including Jung and myself. In his autobiography Jung describes two of his own dreams regarding Self and ego. One, soon after his near-fatal heart attack in 1944, was of a yogi in meditation. With a start he saw that the yogi had Jung's own face! If the yogi awakened from his trance, he, Jung, would vanish![15]

The second dream occurred some fifteen years later. In Jung's paper on flying saucers, he hypothesized that UFOs are our projection of the Self. His own dream was of three UFOs over the lake of Zürich . The third one rotated vertically. It was a giant lens attached to a magic lantern aimed directly at Jung. In effect, Jung saw himself as object to the UFO as subject. Thus Jung is moved to comment:

> We always think the UFOs are projections of ours. Now it turns out that we are their projections. I am projected by the magic lantern as C.G. Jung. But who manipulates the apparatus?[16]

4. A Socratic methodology, drawing material primarily from the client. The analyst's personality is not hidden or masked and feelings for one another are freely exchanged.

This involves a de-emphasis on the transference/counter-transference, with a tendency to see the analyst and analysand as allies in dealing with the analysand's unconscious. Analysis is an empathetic, face-to-face, "I-Thou"

---

[15] *Memories, Dreams, Reflections,* pp. 323f.

[16] "Flying Saucers: A Modern Myth," *Civilization in Transition,* CW 10, pars. 605ff..

relationship,[17] which admits of no "technique" except the heartfelt consideration of material provided by the unconscious, especially dreams.

corollary l—Friendship is a natural terminus of analysis.

All my analysts became friends. Bingham Dai, my first analyst, was a Chinese sociologist trained by Harry Stack Sullivan. Two years after I left Duke I wrote Dr Dai. I would be passing through Durham and would like to see him. He replied "I'm always glad to see a former pupil." Pupil! With that word he recast our relationship as teacher-pupil. It was the most rapid and elegant resolution of the transference I ever experienced. Later I asked him to lecture in Dallas. We then interacted as friends and colleagues.

Rivkah Kluger, my first Jungian analyst, ended our first session with tea and cookies. Several years later she seemed distracted during one of my hours. I asked why. Her doctor had advised hysterectomy. She was in a quandary, could focus on nothing else. We spent the rest of the hour largely on her problem. I was pleased that she valued my medical opinion, and she was grateful. She did not bill me for that session.

While immigrating to Israel the Klugers stopped briefly in Zürich. I resumed analysis with Rivkah and helped them change apartments. I last saw her at an IAAP congress in London. We had refreshments at a sidewalk café. There was no significant transference/countertransference. This was true also with Deiter Baumann, my second Jungian analyst, before, during and after my work with him.

Marie-Louise von Franz was my third Jungian analyst. My

---

[17] See Mario Jacoby, *The Analytic Encounter: Transference and Human Relationship,* pp. 61ff.

active imagination of Manjusri both made me aware of and resolved my transference.[18] I kept up our friendship via mail and visits to Zürich.

My fourth Jungian analyst was the late Christopher Whitmont. A dream in Zürich suggested him. We both were interested in group therapy. He invited me to sample one of his groups to compare our styles. I did. They were virtually the same. There was no significant transference.

corollary 2—If anything significant is to happen the analyst, too, must be involved in the process.

5. An emphasis on the responsibility of each person for his or her own individuation.

This typically involves withdrawing the projection onto one's analyst as an almighty healer. This process is facilitated by the analyst's candid admission of personal difficulties, complexes, etc., and the frank exchange of feelings.

6. "High carelessness" in the use of the intuitive function, but only after the sensation function has gathered as much data as possible from the analysand-dreamer.

"High carelessness" is how Eileen Garret, the famous American medium (1893-1970), described her successes. This may also be involved in successful dream interpretation. Free-wheeling intuition can come up with breathtaking insights—but also abysmal flops. It needs the help of the other functions: sensation, thinking and feeling.

7. The goal of analysis is seen as growth or "individuation" rather than "cure." Symptoms are seen as symbols of under-

---

[18] See above, p. 64.

lying disruptions in the movement toward wholeness, rather than signs of unfulfilled infantile fantasies and desires.
Conflicts are seldom resolved in terms in which they are first described. The individual begins to see through a larger frame; problems are understood in a new context and transcended.

8. A tendency to see any structures given focal attention as reflecting, through projection, their gestalt in an analogous structure of intrapsychic contents and their gestalt.
Thus, psychological thinking is metaphorical thinking, an ability to recognize a similarity between outer (objective) and inner (subjective) patterns.

9. Considering the inner world to be of equal weight or value as the external world and a belief that both worlds are finally one; that is the alchemical unus mundus.
Accordingly, with each dream a decision must be made whether to interpret it objectively or subjectively—or both.

10. Emphasis on dreams and active imagination rather than on the transference/countertransference.
The need to be alert to this issue was brought home to me by my client Margretta's dream of a white rhinoceros. We were having a session in a pleasant meadow beside a calm lake. In the distance we saw a white rhinoceros approaching. If it was a threat, we would jump in the lake [become unconscious] for safety. On another occasion one of her dreams reminded me of that dream. I asked her, "Does this dream bring to mind your dream of a white rhinoceros?" She looked surprised and replied, "*What* dream of a white rhinoceros? *I* never had such a dream!" In a flash I saw that it had been *my* dream! The

meaning of the dream was apparently that we shared a complex (symbolized by a white rhinoceros) that if activated would threaten us both.

11. Implicit recognition of two forms of the archetypal Self—hierarchical (call it Self-1) and rotational (Self-2).[19]
The major difference between the two forms of the Self—the split of *Christos* and *Diabolos,* good and evil—occurs only in Self-1. It is not found in Self-2.

After I graduated from the Zürich Jung Institute, the first few IAAP congresses I attended began to resemble church retreats. The same tired dogmas were revivified with fresh new clinical and archetypal examples. The Classic Jungian Tradition, then dominant, needed compensation. This compensation soon appeared in the Developmental Clinical Tradition, originating with the London school. This approach focuses on developmental issues, even intrauterine ones. Clinically the Developmental Tradition focuses on the transference and countertransference. Thus I think of traditions as being absorbed. One's school of psychology is a subjective choice.

The following excerpts from an unpublished survey show the relative influence of the Classic and Developmental Traditions.

Synchronicity: A Scarab Survey

---

[19] See my chapter "Jung's Aionic Self" in P. Howell and J. Hall, eds., *Self Through Art and Science.*

The Synchronicity Committee, composed of Jungian analysts, parapsychologists and others, was formed several years ago to discuss synchronicity, collect a database of synchronicities, and edit a book on the subject. The Synchronicity Committee received a grant from the IAAP to further these projects. A survey form was run in the newsletters of the IAAP and the Umbrella Group in the UK. Surprisingly, no responses were received, not one. Then the research committee, composed of Roderick Main, Jan Marlan and myself, simplified the questionnaire and solicited responses in the AGAP (Zürich graduates) newsletter, receiving better results.

About this time, Roderick Main, while lecturing on synchronicity, asked his audience to conduct a thought experiment by imaging themselves in Jung's famous example. Jung was discussing with a woman her dream of a piece of scarab jewelry when he noticed a scarab beetle tapping at the window as if trying to fly into the room. Jung opened the window, caught the insect, and showed it to the startled dreamer. If you were in Jung's situation what would you do?

After the lecture a female analyst spoke to Roderick, saying "I couldn't possibly do as Jung did, which violates a basic rule of my training, to stay focused on the transference/counter-transference field."

The Synchronicity Committee then simplified its questionnaire, adding these comments:

> Also, the committee is trying to assess current attitudes toward synchronicity by asking analysts to conduct a "thought experiment."
>
> If you were today in Jung's situation of discussing a patient's dream of a scarab when you noticed a scarab-like beetle tapping at the window as if trying to get in would you—

1. Do essentially as Jung did—catch it and call it to the patient's attention?

2. Do something else. If so, what?

3. Although both are important, which would you emphasize: Symbols from the unconscious (as in the CJT), or transference/countertransference (as in the DCT)?

There were too few responses to support general statements. We have the impression (but *only* an impression) that analysts identifying with the Classic School are more likely to do what Jung did than those emphasizing the Developmental School. This brief preliminary report gives an example of the work of the Synchronicity Committee.

The scarab survey needs a larger database. Please answer the survey questions and mail or email your responses to: James Hall, 9751 Trevor Drive, Dallas TX 75243-2315; tel. 972-664-1141; email: dreamdoc@internetdesk.net.

For various reasons, the other two members of the Research Committee resigned. The Synchronicity Committee itself disbanded. I was left alone. I will report the data. I have helped and will help anyone who will carry forward this interesting study.

At the time of the survey (2005), the CJT response was cited over DCT by less than one percentage point.

May the Classic yin and the Developmental yang continue their close dance, creating "the August Lord of the Center of Heaven," from whom may arise the goal of all our questing—the living stone, the *filius philosophorum.*

C.G.Jung gardening at his Bollingen tower (about 1957).

Suggested Readings in the Classic Jungian Tradition

(See bibliography for publication details)

Alberto Heule

1. By Marie-Louise von Franz: Any of her works, especially:
   Number and Time
   The Problem of the Puer Aeternus
   Redemption Motifs in Fairy Tales
   Shadow and Evil in Fairy Tales
2. By Jung: Any of his *Collected Works* (CW), especially:
   "The Transcendent Function" in CW 8
   "The Psychology of the Transference" in CW 16
   Diagrams of the Self in the penultimate chapter of *Aion* (CW 9ii)
   Memories, Dreams, Reflections
3. About Jung
   Hannah, Barbara, *Jung: His Life and Work*
   von Franz, *C.G. Jung: His Myth in Our Time*
4. In the Classic Jungian Tradition [CJT]
   Boa, Fraser, and von Franz, *The Way of the Dream*
   Hall, James A., *Jungian Dream Interpretation*
   Hall, James A., *The Jungian Experience: Analysis and Individuation*
   Hall, James A. "The Unconscious Christian: The Image of God in Dreams"
   Hall, James A., "Jung's Aionic Self." In Hall, J.A., and Howell, Patton, eds., *Self Through Art and Science*
   Hillman, James, *Insearch*
   Jacobi, Jolande, *Complex/Archetype/Symbol*
   Whitmont, Edward C., *The Symbolic Quest*

5. Jung and the Western Esoteric Tradition [W.E.T.]
   Fielding, Charles, *The Practical Quabalah*
6. Jung and the "East"
   Coward, H.G., *Jung and Yoga*
7. Jung and Taoism
   Stiskin, Menahum Nahum, *The Looking Glass God: A Study in Yin and Yang*

Books that helped me:

8. Relevant nonfiction
   Fingarette, Herbert, *The Self in Transformation*
   Fromm, Erich, *Escape from Freedom*
   James, William, *The Will to Believe*
   Polanyi, Michael, *Personal Knowledge*
9. Relevant fiction
   Camus, Albert, *The Rebel*
   Hudson, William Henry, *Green Mansions*
   Heule, Alberto, *The Last Initiation of the Ancient Order of the Stellar Sun* (Forthcoming)
   Moore, Christopher, *Lamb*
   Wolfe, Thomas, *Look Homeward, Angel*
10. Relevant poetry
   Eliot, T.S., *Complete Poems and Plays, 1909-1950.*
   Hall, James A., *Complete Poems and Plays 1948-2008* (Forthcoming)
   Houseman, A. E., *A Shropshire Lad*

[See the bibliography and final pages of this volume for other relevant works.—Ed.]

Contributors

Joan Juliet Buck is an American-born journalist and novelist. She was the editor-in-chief of French *Vogue* from 1994-2001. Before that, she was an editor for British *Vogue.* A contributing editor for *Vanity Fair* since 1988, she began her career at Condé Nast Publications in 1968. She is the author of *The Only Place To Be* (1982).

Barbara Davies. See above, page 75.

James A. Hall. See above, page 75.

Robert S. Henderson is a pastoral psychotherapist in Glaston-bury, Connecticut. He and his wife, Janis, also a psycho-therapist, are co-authors of *Living with Jung: "Enterviews" with Jungian Analysts, vol. 1* (Spring Journal and Books). (Volumes 2 and 3 are forthcoming.*)* Many of their interviews with Jungian analysts have been published in *Psychological Perspectives, Spring Journal, Quadrant, Harvest* and the *San Francisco Jung Library Journal.*

Alberto Heule is an itinerant Jungian counselor.

Thomas B. Kirsch, M.D., is a graduate of the C.G. Jung Institute, San Francisco (1968), past president of the C.G. Jung Institute of San Francisco, and past president of the Inter-national Association for Analytical Psychology (IAAP). He is the author of *The Jungians: A Comparative and Historical Perspective* (2000), and co-editor of *Initiation: The Living Reality of an Archetype* (2007). In process: *Corres-pondence between C.G. Jung and James Kirsch.*

Anne Maguire, M.D., is an Analytical Psychologist of the school of Jung, trained in Zürich. She practices in England.

She is a Specialist Physician and Dermatologist, and a fellow of the Royal College of Physicians, London. She has written three books on Psychosomatic Medicine and numerous articles in diverse journals. She lectures widely, chiefly in Europe. She is the author of *Hauterkrankungen als Botschaften der Selle* (The Fire and the Serpent; *Vom Sinn der Kranke Sinne* (The Meaning of the Sick Senses); and *Die dunklen Begleiter der Selle* (Seven Deadly Sins: The Dark Companions of the Soul).

Daryl Sharp, B.Sc., B.J., M.A., is a graduate of Carleton University in Ottawa, Canada, and the University of Sussex in Brighton, England. He is a diplomate of the C.G. Jung Institute in Zürich (1978) and general editor and publisher of Inner City Books (Studies in Jungian Psychology by Jungian Analysts). He is the author of seventeen books in the Inner City series, including *Personality Types: Jung's Model of Typology* (1986), *Digesting Jung: Food for the Journey* (2001), and the ongoing series *Jung Uncorked: Rare Vintages from the Cellar of Analytical Psychology* (vols. 1 and 2, 2008, and forthcoming). He lives in Toronto, Canada, where he is past president of the Ontario Association of Jungian Analysts and active in the training program of the Ontario Association of Jungian Analysts.

Bibliography

Arberry, A.J., ed. *Persian Poems.* Trans. A.J. Arberry. New York: Everyman, 1954.

Boa, Fraser, and von Franz, Marie-Louise. *The Way of the Dream.* 2nd ed. Boston: Shambhala, 1994.

Buck, Joan Juliet. "On Love, Maturity and Happiness: An Interview with Marie-Louise von Franz, Jung's Foremost Pupil." In *Vogue Magazine.* New York: Condé Nast, November 1986

_____. *The Only Place to Be.* New York: Random House, 1982.

Campbell, Joseph. *This Business of the Gods.* In Conversation with Fraser Boa. Boston: Shambhala, 1994.

Camus, Albert. *The Rebel: An Essay on Man in Revolt.* New York: Vintage Books, 1959.

Coward, H.G. *Jung and Yoga.* New York: Suny Press, 1985.

Edinger, Edward F. *The Aion Lectures: Exploring the Self in Jung's* Aion. Toronto: Inner City Books, 1996.

_____. *The Creation of Consciousness: Jung's Myth for Modern Man.* Toronto: Inner City Books, 1984.

_____. *Ego and Archetype.* New York: Penguin Books, 1973.

_____. *The Mysterium Lectures: A Journey Through Jung's* Mysterium Coniunctionis. Toronto: Inner City Books, 1995.

_____. *The Mystery of the Coniunctio: Alchemical Image of Individuation.* Toronto: Inner City Books, 1994.

_____. *Transformation of the God-Image.* Toronto: Inner City Books, 1992.

Eliot, T.S. *The Complete Poems and Plays, 1909-1950.* New York: Harcourt, Brace & World, 1971.

Fielding, Charles. *The Practical Quabalah.* York Beach, ME: Samuel Weiser Inc., 1989.

Fiertz, H.K. *Jungian Psychiatry.* Zürich: Daimon Verlag, 1992.

Fingarette, Herbert. *The Self in Transformation: Psychoanalysis, Philosophy and the Life of the Spirit.* New York: Harper, 1965.

Freud, Sigmund. *New Introductory Lectures on Psycho-Analysis.* Trans. James Strachey. New York: W.W. Norton, 1965.

Frey-Rohn, Liliane. *From Freud to Jung.* Trans. F.E. Engreen and E.K. Engreen. New York: C.G. Jung Foundation, 1974.

Fromm, Erich. *Escape from Freedom.* New York: Henry Holt and Company, 1994.

Hall, James A. *Jungian Dream Interpretation: A Handbook of Theory and Practice.* Toronto: Inner City Books, 1983.

_____. *The Jungian Experience: Analysis and Individuation.* Toronto: Inner City Books, 1986.

_____. "Jung's Aionic Self." In *Self Through Art and Science.* Ed. Howell, Patton, and Hall, James.

Hall, James, and Howell, Patton. *Locked in to Life.* Boise, Idaho, 2002.

Hall, James, and Meckel, Daniel J. *The Unconscious Christian: The Image of God in Dreams.* New York: Paulist Press, 1993.

Hannah, Barbara. *The Cat, Dog and Horse Lectures, and "The Beyond."* Ed. Dean L. Frantz. Wilmette, IL: Chiron Publications, 1992.

_____. *Encounters with the Soul: Active Imagination as developed by C.G. Jung.* Boston: Sigo Press, 1981.

_____. *Jung: His Life and Work (A Biographical Memoir).* New York: G.P. Putnam's Sons, 1976.

_____. *The Inner Journey: Essays on Jungian Psychology.* Toronto: Inner City Books, 2000.

Hillman, James. *Insearch: Psychology and Religion.* New York: Charles Scribner's Sons, 1967.

Houseman, A.E. "A Shropshire Lad." In *The Collected Poems of A.E. Houseman.* London, UK: Wordsworth Poetry Library, 2005.

Howell, Patton, and Hall, James, eds. *Self Through Art and Science.* Bloomington, IN: First Books, 2001.

Hudson, William Henry. *Green Mansions: A Romance of the Tropical Forest.* New York, BiblioBazaar, 2007.

Jacobi, Jolande. *Complex/Archetype/Symbol in the Psychology of C.G. Jung* (Bollingen Series LVII). Trans. Ralph Manheim. Princeton: Princeton University Press, 1959.

Jacoby, Mario. *The Analytic Encounter: Transference and Human Relationship.* Toronto: Inner City Books, 1984.

Jaffé, Aniela. *C.G. Jung: Word and Image.* (Bollingen Series XCVII.2). Princeton: Princeton University Press, 1983.

_____. *Death Dreams and Ghosts: An Archetypal Approach.* Foreword by C.G. Jung. Zürich : Daimon Verlag, 1999.

_____. *The Myth of Meaning in the Work of C.G. Jung.* Zürich: Daimon Verlag, 1984.

_____. *Was Jung a Mystic? And Other Essays.* Zürich: Daimon Verlag, 1989.

James, William. *The Will to Believe.* New York: Longman, 1912.

Jung, *C.G. The Collected Works* (Bollingen Series XX). 20 vols. Trans. R.F.C. Hull. Ed. H. Read, M. Fordham, G. Adler, Wm. McGuire. Princeton: Princeton University Press, 1953-1979.

_____. *Letters* (Bollingen Series XCV). 2 vols. Trans. R.F.C. Hull. Ed. G. Adler, A. Jaffé. Princeton: Princeton University Press, 1973.

_____. *Memories, Dreams, Reflections.* Ed. Aniela Jaffé. New York: Vintage Books, 1965.

Jung, C.G., and von Franz, Marie-Louise, eds. *Man and His Symbols.* London: Aldus Books, 1964.

Jung, C.G. and Wilhelm, Richard. *The Secret of the Golden Flower.* Trans. R. Wilhelm and C. Baynes. London: Routledge and Kegan Paul, 1962.

Jung, Emma. *Animus and Anima: Two Essays.* Woodstock, CT: Spring Publications, 1985.

Jung, Emma, and von Franz, Marie-Louise. *The Grail Legend.* Trans. Andrea Dykes. Boston: Sigo Press, 1986.

Kennedy-Xipolitas, Emmanuel, ed. *The Fountain of the Love of Wisdom: An Homage to Marie-Louise von Franz.* Wilmette, IL: Chiron Publications, 2006.

Kiley, Dan. *The Peter Pan Syndrome: Men Who Have Never Grown up.* New York: Dodd Mean, 1983.

Kirsch, Thomas B. *The Jungians: A Comparative and Historical Perspective.* Philadelphia: Taylor & Francis, Inc., 2000.

Kirsch, Thomas B., Beane, Virginia, and Singer, Thomas, eds. *Initiation: The Living Reality of an Archetype.* New York: Routledge, 2007.

Kluger, Rivkah Schärf. *The Archetypal Significance of Gilgamesh: A Modern Ancient Hero.* Zürich: Daimon Verlag, 1991.

_____. *Psyche in Scripture: The Idea of the Chosen People and Other Essays.* Toronto: Inner City Books, 1995.

Koller, John M. and Koller, Patricia Joyce. *Asian Philosophies.* Third ed. Upper Saddle River, NJ: Prentice Hall, 1998.

Meier, C.A. *Ancient Incubation and Modern Psychotherapy.* Evanston, IL: Northwestern University Press, 1967.

_____. *Healing Dream and Ritual.* Zürich : Daimon Verlag, 1998.

_____. *Personality: The Individuation Process in the Light of C.G. Jung's Typology.* Trans. David N. Roscoe. Zürich: Daimon Verlag, 1995.

_____. *The Unconscious in Its Empirical Manifestations.* Trans. E. Rolfe. Boston: Sigo Press, 1984.

Moore, Christopher. *Lamb.* New York: William Morrow, 2002.

Onians, R.B. *The Origins of European Thought.* New York: Arno Press, 1973.

Polanyi, Michael. *Personal Knowledge: Towards a Post-Critical Philosophy.* Chicago: University of Chicago Press, 1958, 1962.

Sharp, Daryl. *Digesting Jung: Food for the Journey.* Toronto: Inner City Books, 2001.

_____. *Jung Uncorked: Rare Vintages from the Cellar of Analytical Psychology.* 2 vols. and forthcoming. Toronto: Inner City Books, 2008.

_____. *Jungian Psychology Unplugged: My Life as an Elephant.* Toronto: Inner City Books, 1998.

_____. *Personality Types: Jung's Model of Typology.* Toronto: Inner City Books, 1987.

_____. *The Secret Raven: Conflict and Transformation in the Life of Franz Kafka.* Toronto: Inner City Books, 1980.

_____. *Who Am I, Really? Personality, Soul and Individuation.* Toronto: Inner City Books, 1995.

Sparks, J. Gary: *At the Heart of Matter: Synchronicity and Jung's Spiritual Testament.* Toronto: Inner City Books, 2007.

Stevens, Anthony. *Archetype Revisited: An Updated Natural History of the Self.* Toronto: Inner City Books, 2003.

Stiskin, Menahum Nahum. *The Looking Glass God: A Study in Yin and Yang.* Kyoto, Japan: Autumn Press, 1971.

van der Post, Laurens and Pottiez, Jean-Marc. *A Walk with a White Bushman.* New York: William Morrow, 1986.

van der Post, Laurens and Taylor, Jane. *Testament to the Bushman.* Middlesex, U.K.: Penguin Books, 1985.

von Franz, Marie-Louise. *Alchemical Active Imagination.* Zürich: Spring Publications, 1979.

_____. *Alchemy: An Introduction to the Symbolism and the Psychology*. Toronto: Inner City Books, 1980.

_____. *Animus and Anima in Fairy Tales.* Toronto: Inner City Books, 2002.

_____. *Archetypal Dimensions of the Psyche.* Boston: Shambhala, 1997.

_____. *Archetypal Patterns in Fairy Tales.* Toronto: Inner City Books, 1997.

_____, ed., with commentary. *Aurora Consurgens: A document attributed to Thomas Aquinas on the problem of opposites in alchemy*. Trans. R.F.C. Hull and A.S.B. Glover. Toronto: Inner City Books, 2000.

_____. *C.G. Jung: His Myth in Our Time.* Toronto: Inner City Books, 1998.

_____. *The Cat: A Tale of Feminine Redemption.* Toronto: Inner City Books, 1999.

_____. *Creation Myths.* Zürich: Spring Publications, 1972.

_____. *The Feminine in Fairy Tales.* Zürich: Spring Publications, 1972.

_____. *Muhammad ibn Umail's Hall Ar-Rumuz* (Clearing of Enigmas). Foreword by Theodor Abt. Private edition. Egg, Switzerland: Fotorotar AG, 1999.

_____. *Individuation in Fairy Tales.* Zürich: Spring Publications, 1971.

_____. *Introduction to the Interpretation of Fairy Tales.* Zürich: Spring Publications, 1970.

_____. *Number and Time: Reflections Leading Towards a Unification of Psychology and Physics*. Trans. A. Dykes. Evanston, IL: Northwestern University Press, 1974.

_____. *On Divination and Synchronicity: The Psychology of Meaningful Chance.* Toronto: Inner City Books, 1980.

_____. *On Dreams & Death: A Jungian Interpretation.* Foreword by Emmanuel Kennedy-Xipolitas. Trans. E. Kennedy-Xipolitas, Vernon Brooks. La Salle, IL: Open Court, 1998.

_____. *The Passion of Perpetua: A Psychological Interpretation of Her Visions.* Toronto: Inner City Books, 2004.

_____. *The Problem of the Puer Aeternus.* Third edition. Ed. Daryl Sharp. Toronto: Inner City Books, 2000.

_____. The Process of Individuation," in Jung, C.G., and von Franz Marie-Louise, eds., *Man and His Symbols.* London: Aldus Books, 1964.

_____. *Projection and Re-Collection in Jungian Psychology: Reflec-tions of the Soul.* Trans. W.H. Kennedy. La Salle, IL: Open Court, 1980.

_____. *Psyche and Matter.* Boston: Shambhala, 1992.

_____. *A Psychological Interpretation of* The Golden Ass *of Apuleius.* Zürich: Spring Publications, 1970.

_____. *Psychotherapy.* Boston: Shambhala, 1993.

_____. *Redemption Motifs in Fairy Tales.* Toronto: Inner City Books, 1980.

_____. *Shadow and Evil in Fairy Tales.* Zürich: Spring Publications, 1974.

_____. *The Visions of Bruder Klaus.* Zürich: Daimon Verlag, 1986.

Von Franz, Marie-Louise, and Boa, Fraser. *The Way of the Dream.* Boston: Shambhala, 1994.

Von Franz, Marie-Louise, and Hillman, James. *Lectures on Jung's Typology.* Zürich: Spring Publications, 1971.

Wilhelm, Richard, trans. *The I Ching or Book of Changes.* Trans. C.F. Baynes. London: Routledge and Kegan Paul, 1968.

Wilhelm, Richard and Wilhelm, Helmut. *Understanding the I Ching* (Bollingen Series XIX:2). Princeton: Princeton University Press, 1988.

Whitmont, Edward C. *The Symbolic Quest: Basic Concepts of Analytical Psychology.* Princeton: Princeton University Press, 1978.

Wolfe, Thomas. *Look Homeward, Angel.* New York: Simon & Schuster, 1995.

Woodman, Marion. *Addiction to Perfection: The Still Unravished Bride.* Toronto: Inner City Books, 1982.

_____. The Owl Was a Baker's Daughter: Obesity, Anorexia Nervosa and the Repressed Feminine. Toronto: Inner City Books, 1980.

Index (Numbers in *italics* refer to illustrations)

Also in this Series, by Marie-Louise von Franz

AURORA CONSURGENS: On the Problem of Opposites in Alchemy
ISBN 978-0-919123-90-8. (2000) 576pp. **30-page Index** ***Sewn*** $50
A penetrating commentary on a rare medieval treatise, scattered throughout with insights relevant to the process of individuation in modern men and women.

THE PROBLEM OF THE PUER AETERNUS
ISBN 978-0-919123-88-5. (2000) 288pp. **11 illustrations** ***Sewn*** $40
The term *puer aeternus* (Latin, eternal youth) is used in Jungian psychology to describe a certain type of man or woman: charming, creative, ever in pursuit of their dreams. This is the classic study of those who remain adolescent into their adult years.

THE CAT: A Tale of Feminine Redemption
ISBN 978-0-919123-84-7. (1999) 128pp. **8 illustrations** ***Sewn*** $25
"The Cat" is a Romanian fairy tale about a young princess who is bewitched—turned into a cat. . . . One by one, von Franz unravels the symbolic threads.

C.G. JUNG: His Myth in Our Time
ISBN 978-0-919123-78-6. (1998) 368pp. **30-page Index** *Sewn* $40
The most authoritative biography of Jung, comprising an historical account of his seminal ideas on the collective unconscious, archetypes and complexes, typology, creativity, active imagination and individuation.

ARCHETYPAL PATTERNS IN FAIRY TALES
ISBN 978-0-919123-77-9. (1997) 192pp. *Sewn* $30
In-depth studies of six fairy tales—from Spain, Denmark, China, France and Africa, and one from the Grimm collection.

REDEMPTION MOTIFS IN FAIRY TALES
ISBN 978-0-919123-01-4. (1980) 128pp. *Sewn* $25
A nonlinear approach to the significance of fairy tales for an understanding of the process of psychological development. A modern classic.

ON DIVINATION AND SYNCHRONICITY: Psychology of Meaningful Chance
ISBN 978-0-919123-02-1. (1980) 128pp. **15 illustrations** *Sewn* $25
A penetrating study of the psychological aspects of time, number and methods of divining fate such as the I Ching, astrology, Tarot, palmistry, dice, etc. Extends Jung's views and contrasts Western attitudes with those of the East.

ALCHEMY: An Introduction to the Symbolism and the Psychology
ISBN 978-0-919123-04-5. (1980) 288pp. **84 illustrations** *Sewn* $40

Designed as an introduction to Jung's weightier writings on alchemy. Invaluable for understanding dream images and relationships. Rich in insights from experience.

Also by in this Series, by Daryl Sharp

Please see last page for discounts and postage/handling.

THE SECRET RAVEN
Conflict and Transformation in the Life of Franz Kafka
ISBN 978-0-919123-00-7. (1980) 128 pp. $25

PERSONALITY TYPES: Jung's Model of Typology
ISBN 978-0-919123-30-9. (1987) 128 pp. **Diagrams** $25

THE SURVIVAL PAPERS: Anatomy of a Midlife Crisis
ISBN 978-0-919123-34-2. (1988) 160 pp. $25

DEAR GLADYS: The Survival Papers, Book 2
ISBN 978-0-919123-36-6. (1989) 144 pp. $25

JUNG LEXICON: A Primer of Terms and Concepts
ISBN 978-0-919123-48-9. (1991) 160 pp. **Diagrams** $25

GETTING TO KNOW YOU: The Inside Out of Relationship
ISBN 978-0-919123-56-4. (1992) 128 pp. $25

THE BRILLIG TRILOGY:

1. **CHICKEN LITTLE: The Inside Story *(A Jungian romance)***
ISBN 978-0-919123-62-5. (1993) 128 pp. $25

2. **WHO AM I, REALLY? Personality, Soul and Individuation**
ISBN 978-0-919123-68-7. (1995) 144 pp. $25

3. **LIVING JUNG: The Good and the Better**
ISBN 978-0-919123-73-1. (1996) 128 pp. $25

JUNGIAN PSYCHOLOGY UNPLUGGED: My Life as an Elephant
ISBN 978-0-919123-81-6. (1998) 160 pp. $25

DIGESTING JUNG: Food for the Journey
ISBN 978-0-919123-96-0. (2001) 128 pp. $25

JUNG UNCORKED: Rare Vintages from the Cellar of Analytical Psychology
Two books. ISBN 978-1-894574-21-1/22-8.. (2008) 128 pp. cach. $25 each

THE SLEEPNOT TRILOGY:

1. **NOT THE BIG SLEEP: On having fun, seriously *(A Jungian romance)***
ISBN 978-0-894574-13-6. (2005) 128 pp. $25

2. **ON STAYING AWAKE: Getting Older and Bolder** *(Another Jungian romance)*
ISBN 978-0-894574-16-7. (2006) 144 pp. $25

3. **EYES WIDE OPEN: Late Thoughts** *(Another Jungian romance)*
ISBN 978-0-894574-18-1.. (2007) 160 pp. $25